Reconstructing the Lifelong Learner

This interesting examination of adult learning for change illustrates through diverse case studies and theoretical perspectives that personal change is inextricably linked to broader organisational and social change.

The authors explore how theorising education as a vehicle for self-change impacts on the practices of educators, learning specialists and others concerned with promoting learning for change.

The book explores the relationship between pedagogy, identity and change and illustrates this through a range of case studies focusing on the following:

- Self-help books
- Work-based learning
- Corporate culture training
- HIV/AIDS education
- Gender education
- Sex offender education

The study culminates with an exploration of how the practice of writing an academic text has itself contributed to the identities of the authors.

This unique text will be of interest to students of education, sociology, cultural studies and change management as well as teachers and educators and professionals involved in lifelong learning or change management in any way.

Clive Chappell and **Nicky Solomon** are Co-Directors, and **Carl Rhodes** is Senior Research Fellow, of OVAL Research in the Faculty of Education, University of Technology Sydney.

Mark Tennant and **Lyn Yates** are Professors in Education at the University of Technology Sydney.

Reconstructing the Lifelong Learner

Pedagogy and identity in individual, organisational and social change

Clive Chappell, Carl Rhodes, Nicky Solomon, Mark Tennant and Lyn Yates

RoutledgeFalmer
Taylor & Francis Group

LONDON AND NEW YORK

First published 2003 by RoutledgeFalmer
11 New Fetter Lane, London EC4P 4EE

Simultaneously published in the USA and Canada
by RoutledgeFalmer
29 West 35th Street, New York, NY 10001

RoutledgeFalmer is an imprint of the Taylor & Francis Group

© 2003 Clive Chappell, Carl Rhodes, Nicky Solomon, Mark
Tennant and Lyn Yates

Typeset in 10.5/13pt Sabon by Graphicraft Ltd., Hong Kong
Printed and bound in Great Britain by T J International Ltd,
Padstow, Cornwall

British Library Cataloguing in Publication Data
A catalogue record for this book is available from the British
Library

Library of Congress Cataloging in Publication Data
A catalog record has been requested

ISBN 0-415-26348-4 (pbk)
      0-415-26347-6 (hbk)

Contents

Acknowledgements

This book arises out of our long standing interest in changing forms of contemporary education, work and identity. The pursuit of these interests has been supported in various forms by the University of Technology Sydney (UTS). Within UTS this includes the Faculty of Education, the Research in Adult and Vocational Learning (RAVL) research group and the Key University Research Centre in Organisational, Vocational and Adult Learning (OVAL Research). In 2000 RAVL hosted an international conference in Sydney entitled 'Working Knowledge'. This was a key event in terms of being a forum for the presentation of ground-breaking work in the area from around the world. For us it also played a critical part in surfacing the questions and issues that subsequently became the themes of this book. To all of our colleagues at UTS, the Faculty of Education, RAVL, OVAL Research and the Working Knowledge conference we would like to acknowledge the support, encouragement and intellectual stimulation that have been integral in the inspiration for and production of this book. In bringing this together, we also single out Mark Tennant for his initial idea for the book, for getting the project up and running, and for seeing it through to its completion.

In part, the work in this book has been developed in conjunction with an ongoing research project investigating 'Changing Work, Changing Workers, Changing Selves: A Study of Pedagogies in the New Vocationalism', funded by a three year Discovery Grant (2002–4) from the Australian Research Council (ARC).

The authors of this book are members of two research groups based at UTS: Clive Chappell, Carl Rhodes, Nicky Solomon and Mark Tennant are members of OVAL Research and Lyn Yates is a member of CKCI (Changing Knowledges, Changing Identities). Thanks go to the research groups for their ongoing financial and intellectual support.

We thank Julie Gustavs from the Work-Based Learning Unit, in the University of Technology Sydney's Faculty of Business for use of the educational materials, and for conversations regarding work-based learning pedagogy. Julie's assistance was instrumental in the development of Chapter 5. We also wish to acknowledge the assistance given to us by Michael Coffey, coordinator of the HIV/AIDS education program referred to in Chapter 7. Finally, we thank Maree Joulian for the very professional way in which she prepared the manuscript for submission to the editor.

Parts of Chapter 1 have previously been published in M. Tennant (1998) 'Adult education as a technology of the self', *International Journal of Lifelong Education*, 13(4): 364–76 and M. Tennant (2000) 'Adult learning for self development and change', in A. Wilson and E. Hayes, *Handbook 2000: Adult and Continuing Education*, pp. 87–100, Jossey-Bass.

Introduction

The five of us who have written this book have been drawn to this collaboration by a belief that identity is an important frame for examining pedagogy, change and lifelong learning today. We come with different backgrounds, different institutional histories, different theoretical allegiances, and have different practical engagements. But we were interested in talking more to each other about the questions and case studies that are the subject of this book. We hope that the book might also be of interest to others who work in some part of the broad terrain that encompasses pedagogy, lifelong learning, organisational and social change.

Our approach to planning and writing this book was to have broad ranging discussions about our theoretical and practical interests and how these relate to the purpose of the book. Once the structure and purpose of the book was settled, the initial drafts for each of the chapters were individually assigned. Then followed iterations of group critique, redrafting, and repositioning of each of the chapters within the book as a whole.

As might be expected, this process surfaced both our commonalities and differences. At the most general level we recognise that we are people who are engaged in certain types of 'abstract' theorising around educational issues as well as people who are engaged in 'how do we practice' type issues (as teachers, reformers, administrators and so on). In addition we share a belief that looking at pedagogies through a focus on technologies of the self, and constructing/constructed identities is an interesting and important thing to do right now.

Where we are most differentiated is in our different disciplinary and workplace histories which, not surprisingly, produce different senses of what are the key issues or modes for doing analysis and practice. But it is also interesting that from such diverse disciplinary backgrounds we found a common project around questions of identity, change and pedagogy.

In our discussions, for example, we realised that we all share a concern with contemporary forms of education and training that in many ways are informed by diverse but interrelated sets of theorisations of change. We all recognised the influence that new economic times discourses were having on all areas of education, in particular the rise of new vocationalism. We also noted the current interest in new forms of identity and the construction of *self* and the contemporary reconceptualisation of *knowledge* occurring both inside and outside educational institutions.

At a broad theoretical level, we also shared the view that much analysis today converges on the changed demands being placed on learners, and this leads to new significance being placed on concepts of 'self' and 'identity' in understanding contemporary social forms such as education and work. Indeed, new educational outcomes appear to be focused as much upon the characteristics, subjectivity and orientations of the person as on skills and knowledge as more traditionally understood, and this shift has been paralleled by notable shifts of focus among theorists.

Collectively we recognised that among sociologists (e.g. Giddens 1991; Bernstein 1996; du Gay 1996a; Rose 1996) new interest in identity and the 'technology of the self' has emerged as a key issue in understanding the social. We also noted that in psychology too, the rise of 'critical psychology' (Henriques *et al.* 1984) is a related recognition of the socially shaped demands in contemporary psychology, of how individuals experience themselves and their interests. Indeed we felt that all of these theories of identity and the self widely found in contemporary research have developed new sensitivities in the study of educational programmes (Yates 1998, 1999, 2001; Yates and McLeod 2000).

As a result of these shared concerns we felt that 'changing selves' seems to be an *aim* of contemporary education and training and 'changing selves' is also an important lens for analysing educational *processes*, for theorising new social developments, for investigating the ongoing relationship between pedagogy and learner identity (Usher and Solomon 1999) and for investigating the effectiveness of pedagogical programmes.

Each of us has engaged for some time on these interrelated issues as they shape particular aspects of contemporary education. One key interest has been in the pedagogies of adult education seen as 'technologies of the self', and the analysis of pedagogical techniques relative to these questions of broader shifts in society and in the shaping of the individual. Another related interest has been the formation of the working identities of contemporary educational practitioners and the significance of particular institutional contexts on identity construction. A third interest has been in a cross-disciplinary and policy-related critique and elaboration of 'working knowledge' in new work-based contexts that is particularly attuned to insights gained from discourse analysis of documents and texts. A fourth interest has been a study of young people at school, with a particular focus on identities and future trajectories developed in the interaction of particular types of subjectivities and particular school sites and programmes. A fifth interest has been a conceptualisation of organisational learning and the construction of identity through narrative.

Finally, despite our particular interests and theoretical positioning, we share the view that one way of understanding lifelong learning at this contemporary moment is that it foregrounds learning and pedagogy, not merely to make people more skilled or more rounded citizens, but to construct identities that can 'perform better'. This in itself is a very different take on the concept of lifelong learning, which is more usually associated with policy frameworks and instruments designed to reform national education and training systems.

While the contemporary resurgence of lifelong learning is primarily seen as addressing issues such as economic competitiveness in a global marketplace, social inclusion and social cohesion, it can also be seen as a response to the features of contemporary life. Features such as continuous change and uncertainty, the erosion of traditional life trajectories, the need to negotiate one's life more reflexively and the pluralisation of individual and collective identities are all related to structural changes in society resulting from globalising processes and the application of new information technologies.

Edwards *et al.* (2002: 527) argue that a critical form of lifelong learning requires the development of reflexivity:

> While there has been much debate about the nature, extent and significance of lifelong learning as a policy goal, there has been little theoretical discussion specifically of the nature of the learning required to engage with the change processes to which it is meant to be a response . . . We want to suggest that while policies for lifelong learning focus on the accumulation of skills and qualifications as an adaptation to change and uncertainty, a less passive notion

of learning, one more consonant with the needs of civic participation and of agents capable of autonomously generating change
for themselves, requires the development of reflexivity . . . Our
contention here is that in order to engage with the (dis)locations
associated with change processes, learning itself needs to become
reflexive . . . it is through self and social questioning (reflexivity)
that people are able to engage with and (en)counter – affected by
but also affect – contemporary uncertainties.

Edwards *et al.* see reflexivity as 'the capacity to develop critical awareness of the assumptions that underlie practices' (p. 533) and they
follow Eraut (2000) in recognising learning as the 'transformation
of understanding, identity and agency' (p. 532). Indeed we believe the
analysis of Edwards *et al.* nicely aligns lifelong learning with the core
concerns of this book: pedagogical practices, change and identity.

The case studies in this book are written in a spirit of 'look at what
is happening here' from the perspective of 'technologies of the self';
and 'look at what is being assumed of and done to learners here in
terms of identity'. To examine this is not to assume that each programme we discuss is 'a bad thing' or that there are ways to proceed
that avoid governance of some type. Indeed, what we are suggesting
is that all pedagogical work is always and everywhere *identity work*
of some kind.

In one sense, our goal has been to create a text that retells the story
of pedagogy in a way that brings identity to the fore in order to
question and explore the relationship between the two. We see our
(reflexive) role in this process as being an active one – i.e. whereas
identity is often not a key construct through which pedagogy is
understood, we wish to place it at the very forefront of a discussion
of pedagogy. As we have tried to demonstrate above, identity can be
made quite explicit as a significant element of pedagogy. Further, we
believe that doing so can be a productive way to understand pedagogy in that it draws attention to its existential rather than its tele-
ological, processual or technical aspects. Thus we are not providing
a handbook of pedagogical techniques, but are more interested in
unsettling pedagogy so that its contemporary formations can be understood and developed.

The book comprises ten chapters. The first three are designed to
introduce various notions of, and relationships between, identity,
pedagogy and change. Chapters 4 to 9 provide a series of case studies
which tease out how this triumvirate of concepts can be used to

critically understand particular examples of contemporary pedagogical practices. Finally, Chapter 10 closes the book by making some general comments on the possible implications of the book as a whole. This structure is designed to help provide entry points into the work as a whole rather than to suggest that the book should be read in a linear fashion, starting with Chapter 1 and moving slowly until the end of the final chapter is reached. We have tried to assemble the book in a way such that any chapter (with the possible exception of Chapter 10) can be read either independently or in conjunction with any other chapter. As ever, of course, the choice is with the reader. Below we provide a brief synopsis of the chapters.

In Chapter 1, 'Education as a site for self-work', we start out by putting forward a case for the relationship between education and identity. This discussion seeks to establish that changing learner identities is (implicitly or explicitly) a part of many forms of educational practice and that such pedagogies contain within them theorisations concerning the self. In following this line, the chapter's purpose is twofold: first to make the general case that education, especially for adults, invariably involves an element of self-formation and change; and second to review and discuss the practices and theories of different traditions in education with a view to identifying their key pedagogical and theoretical issues *vis-à-vis* identity formation.

Whereas the focus of the first chapter is on self-change in relation to pedagogical traditions, in the second chapter, 'Theorising identity', we change our focus to examine the history of the notion of identity *per se*. This chapter thus tries to position our discussion within long-standing and continuing debates on the very nature of identity. The position we take is based on a critique of modernist conceptions of identity, in particular those that focus attention on the knowing, conscious self-sufficient subject; the power of social relations in identity formation; and the relationship between self and society. In providing this critique we also outline what has come to be known as a 'poststructuralist' perspective – one that suggests the increasing pluralisation of society has challenged any pretence that universal and normative frames of reference can provide unchanging anchoring points for identity.

Chapter 3, 'Understanding identity as narrative', concludes the introductory section of the book with a more detailed discussion of how a plural form of identity can be theorised. In particular, the chapter outlines the notion of narrative identity. This discussion is used to suggest that narrative offers a means of understanding identity that accounts for its political dimensions – as manifested in 'identity politics'. This discussion on narrative identity is presented with specific reference to its pedagogical implications.

These first three chapters explore some general theoretical orientations to identity – in terms of its relationships to pedagogical traditions, historical notions of the self and narrative and identity politics. The following six chapters present a range of case studies on the relationships between specific pedagogies and identity formation and change. In choosing the topics for these chapters we have drawn on our diverse experience in order to look broadly at the variety of pedagogies that are in play at different educational sites and within different educational practices as they relate to adult learning. We have drawn examples from a variety of recent or emerging educational practices and sites that are significantly more socially distributed than those traditionally considered as being 'education': self-help books (Chapter 4); work-based learning as a new form of university education (Chapter 5); corporate culture training (Chapter 6); HIV/AIDS education for homeless youths (Chapter 7); gender education (Chapter 8); and sex offender education (Chapter 9).

It should be noted that we have not tried to mould each case study to a common template that fills in the details of a particular model that we set up in the opening chapters. Our intention is to open up ways of examining pedagogies, and the issues we take up are ones that have generated stimulating perspectives from more than one theorist. By examining such a broad range of sites, we intend to demonstrate that issues of identity are important across different types of education, yet that the way such an identity is played out is different in different contexts, sites and programmes. Not only do the cases themselves represent different types of 'pedagogy', but our discussion of them also represents different takes on what an examination of pedagogy might look like. The cases range from books that an individual might purchase voluntarily to a compulsory re-education programme for offenders; from programmes for accreditation in workplaces or education institutions to strategies that would not normally be thought of as 'pedagogy': programmes of cultural change in organisations, and games for youth workers to use with homeless young people. The discussions range from very concrete descriptions of the micro-details of a particular pedagogical strategy (e.g. in the chapters on self-help books – Chapter 4 – and the HOT game – Chapter 7), to more abstract analyses, such as the attempted monological narrative of the self and the problems with such a conception in the chapter on organisational culture (Chapter 6), and the discussion of portfolios in terms of their textual construction of self in Chapter 5.

Briefly then, Chapter 4, 'Pedagogies for personal change in the "self-help" literature', shows how these texts commonly present a 'self' that needs to be discovered (or rediscovered) but one that also needs quite specific training in order to be a fully successful person. Chapter 5, 'Writing portfolios in a work-based learning programme' looks close-up at a programme where workplace and university supposedly come together to accredit a worker for work-based learning. It discusses identity and change in the context of this new pedagogical framing and draws attention both to the challenges this represents for the institution and to the particular representation of self that is required to be produced textually via a portfolio. Chapter 6, 'Pedagogy as a tool for corporate culture' discusses the contemporary interest in organisational culture as the locus of change and productivity in the workplace, and in particular the conflating of corporate and individual interests and identities that this presumes. It discusses issues of power in relation to claims being made over particular narratives of identity. Chapter 7, 'Games as a pedagogy in HIV/AIDS education' discusses a game that was developed as a pedagogical tool that could be used by youth workers to take up HIV/AIDS awareness with homeless young people. This chapter discusses how the game, considered as a pedagogy, is directed both to the youth worker and to those considered at risk, and assumes rather different stances to their respective identities. Compared with other chapters in the book, the HOT game that is discussed here takes pains *not* to be seen as engaged in identity change for young people, and *not* to be promoting a desired identity. Chapter 8, 'Social movements and programmes of gender change' takes as its case the social movement around women and gender issues that has generated many local examples of pedagogies of change, ranging from 'consciousness-raising' to government-sponsored programmes for women wanting to re-enter the workforce. It discusses the different type of narrative of self that is produced in such programmes and the reflexivity that permeates this movement as well as our analysis of it. Chapter 9, 'Educational programmes for sex offenders', takes up pedagogies for sex offenders and in particular the training manuals addressed to the teachers of such programmes. This chapter, like Chapters 7 and 8, draws attention to identity work and the demands being made of teachers as well as of those whom they teach.

Finally, in Chapter 10, 'Pedagogy, identity, reflexivity', we review the case studies, drawing attention to our general argument that educators can be understood as broadly involved in identity work. Given this, we suggest that it is appropriate and desirable for educators to be reflexive about their work in terms of their own and others' identities. We then proceed to consider the writing of this book (and academic texts in general) as a particular type of pedagogical practice. In the same way that educators may be openly reflexive about their teaching and its pedagogical claims we too attempt to be openly reflexive about our writing and its pedagogical claims.

Chapter 1

Education as a site for self-work

Introduction

Educators, and others with an educational dimension to their work, are frequently engaged in promoting learning for personal change. Sometimes this is made explicit – for example, in programmes which aim to improve self-esteem or self-concept, or which help people discover their 'authentic' self. Sometimes it is more implicit – for example, in programmes which address significant social issues such as gender stereotyping, racial discrimination, migration, domestic violence, environmental concerns and perhaps health issues: the idea being that personal change is inextricably linked to broader social change.

In the workplace too most changes imply a reorientation of people's values or attitudes or the way they see themselves. Recent interest by organisations, for example, in promoting 'cultural change' programmes for personnel suggests that business now regards the personal change of employees as crucial to the achievement of in-creased efficiency and profitability. The idea here is that people who identify with the culture of an organisation are able to produce the sorts of meanings at work that encourage them to act in ways that contribute to the success of the organisation (see du Gay 1996a).

Irrespective of context, we argue here that all programmes de-signed to act as catalysts for personal or professional growth and change contain implicit theorisations concerning the nature of the self, its development or capacity for change, and the way the self relates to others or to society more generally. Such theorisations are a necessary part of our conception of the possibility of self-change and the associated pedagogies deployed for the purpose of change (e.g. Mezirow's notion of perspective transformation – see Mezirow 1990, 1991; Weissner *et al.* 2000). When engaging with these conceptions a number of questions surface: Can we be the sole agents of our own change? If not, to what extent are we dependent on others to effect self-change? What kinds of activities and relationships promote self-change? What theoretical assumptions underpin contemporary understandings about the possibility of self-change? What is the role of the educator in identity work? How does pedagogical practice contribute to learner and teacher identity formation? What political and ethical issues emerge from using pedagogy to change identity? In what ways do pedagogy, identity and change work together? Different pedagogies offer, or at least imply, different responses to these questions and others like them. Other questions may also be asked, or the above questions reframed, to expose different ways of thinking about the issue of self-formation and change. In other words, different theoretical perspectives pose different questions and cast the problematic in different ways.

We suggest that by engaging with theorisations concerning the self and self-change, practitioners are better able to analyse their own assumptions, make explicit their theoretical position, and tailor their pedagogical practices accordingly. The purpose of this book then, is to theorise education as a vehicle for self-change and to explore how such theorising impacts on the practices of educators, 'learning specialists' and others concerned with promoting learning for change. The position adopted throughout is that the various educational and learning 'programmes' are best seen as technologies for constructing particular kinds of people or 'subjects'.

The purpose of this chapter is twofold: first, to make the general case that education invariably involves an element of self-formation and change, and second, to review and analyse the practices and theories of different traditions in education with a view to identifying the key pedagogical and theoretical issues that hinge on the formation of self and self-change. We commence with a brief discussion of the dualism of 'individual and society' as a way of framing existing pedagogical approaches. We then look at perhaps the most pervasive strategy apparent when there is a deliberate focus on learning for self-change and self-work: reflection on experience as a pedagogical tool. We conclude with a brief discussion of teacher-learner relationships and identity work, and how both are implicated in any decision to adopt a particular pedagogical tool.

The dualism of 'individual' and 'society' in pedagogies of change

It is useful to consider various educational interventions for self-change as belonging to and extending the lineage of 'technologies of the self' as elaborated by Foucault. In his essay on 'Technologies of the Self' (Foucault 1988), Foucault traces the development of technologies of the self in Graeco-Roman philosophy and in early Christianity. Technologies of the self (which stand alongside and interact with technologies of production, sign systems and power)

> permit individuals to effect by their own means or with the help of others a certain number of operations on their own bodies and souls, thoughts, conduct and way of being, so as to transform themselves in order to attain a certain state of happiness, purity, wisdom, perfection, or immortality.
>
> (1988: 18)

Foucault is particularly concerned with the notion of 'taking care of oneself' as a precept or imperative which circulated among a number of different doctrines in the period 3 BC–AD 3. This is a theme developed more extensively in *The Care of the Self: The History of Sexuality*, Volume 3. In this text, Foucault refers to the time and effort expended in attending to oneself in antiquity:

> Taking care of oneself is not a rest cure. There is the care of the body to consider, health regimens, physical exercises without overexertion, the carefully measured satisfaction of needs. There are the meditations, the readings, the notes one takes on books or on the conversations one has heard, notes that one reads again later, the recollection of truths that one knows already but that need to be more fully adapted to one's life . . . there are also the talks one has with a confidant, with friends, with a guide or director. Add to this the correspondence in which one reveals the state of one's soul, solicits advice, gives advice to anyone who needs it . . . Around the care of self there developed an entire activity of speaking and writing in which the work of oneself on oneself and communication with others were linked together.
>
> (1986: 51)

Foucault analyses the techniques associated with different doctrines concerned with the care of self: from the practices of Stoic teachers such as the spiritual retreat, meditation, ritual purification and mentoring; to the Christian tradition of confession, disclosure and renunciation of the self. His interest in these techniques (and their contemporary equivalents such as counselling, guidance and education) is how they figure in the transformation of human beings into subjects, and how power can be exercised or resisted through the work of self on self. As Foucault argued earlier:

> There are two meanings of the word subject: subject to someone else by control and dependence, and tied to his own identity by a conscience or self-knowledge. Both meanings suggest a form of power which subjugates and makes subject to . . . it can be said that there are three types of struggles: either against forms of domination (ethnic, social, religious); against forms of exploitation which separate individuals from what they produce; or against that which ties the individual to himself and submits him to others in this way (struggles against subjection, against forms of subjectivity and submission).
>
> (1983: 212)

A similar analysis can be made of existing pedagogical technologies aimed at fostering certain kinds of self-change and transformation. In this regard, Boud (1989) provides a useful framework (also cited by Usher *et al.* 1997). He comments on four pedagogical traditions: the training and efficiency tradition (with its classical scientific self, a kind of self-contained mechanistic learning machine); the self-direction or andragogical tradition (where the self is conceived as individualistic and unitary, capable of rational reflection on experience, and conferring meaning on experience); the learner-centred or humanistic tradition (with the notion of an innate or authentic self which is in a process of 'becoming' in a holistic integration of thinking, feeling and acting); and the critical pedagogy and social action tradition (with its exploited self of 'false consciousness', an inauthentic self which is socially formed and distorted by ideology and oppressive social structures). The problem with the first three of the above is that they accept as given or neutral that which is highly problematic: for example, knowledge and skills are assumed to be neutral rather than socially and culturally constructed; or experience is seen as given, the source of authentic knowledge and not in any way problematic; or there is assumed to be a true self which exists independently of the social realm. In the andragogical and humanistic traditions in particular, the social is something which is cast as oppressive and to be overcome or transcended through technologies which promote self-control, self-direction, self-management, self-knowledge, autonomy, or self-realisation – technologies which are aimed at empowering the individual learner. The andragogical and humanistic traditions support the conventional view that education can lead to a greater awareness of self through cultivating a self which is independent, rational, autonomous, coherent and which has a sense of social responsibility. In this scenario social change is a matter of individuals acting authentically and autonomously: being truly themselves.

Now this view of the self, which is largely informed by humanistic psychology, has been criticised as being overly individualistic: of portraying social problems as largely individual problems with individual solutions, of accepting as given the social world in which the self resides. This version of self-empowerment through the fostering of personal autonomy is seen by critics as illusory: largely because social structures and forces remain unchallenged. At the very least the increasing pluralisation of society has challenged any pretence that universal social and normative frames of reference can provide unchanging anchoring points for identity. Indeed, increasing social and cultural mobility has begun to erode the possibility of developing a self built on any singular and stable socio-cultural community. Ultimately, and ironically, the technologies which enhance autonomy are said to serve the interests of existing social structures and forces. This view is well expressed by Usher *et al.* (1997: 98):

> These traditions make much of empowering the individual learner, yet they have shown themselves to be wide open to hijacking by an individual and instrumental ethic. The psychologism and individualism of humanistic discourse presented as a concern for the 'person' can lead ultimately and paradoxically to a dehumanisation through the substitution of covert for overt regulation under the guise of 'being human', enabling learners to 'open up', and provide access to their 'inner world'. This is an infiltration of power by subjectivity and a complementary infiltration of subjectivity by power.

Such a position is not new in social theory. Indeed, critical pedagogy, and its associated technologies, is based upon a view of the self as socially constituted. Now there are very different versions of how the social becomes a constitutive part of the self: how the 'outside' gets 'inside' so to speak, and how social processes interpenetrate the psyche. Nevertheless they all have in common the notion that the self participates in its own subjugation and domination, whether it is through 'false consciousness' produced by membership of a particular social group, or the internalisation of social 'oppression' through individual 'repression' (in the psychoanalytic sense). But Usher et al., from their postmodernist stance, regard critical pedagogy as reifying the social as a monolithic 'other' which serves to oppress and crush, and they warn that it is a mistake to adopt an over-socialised and over-determined view of the person:

> There is a tendency in the critical tradition to end up with a conception of the self which is, on the one hand, oversocialised and overdetermined and on the other, patronising in so far as selves have to be seen as normally in a state of false consciousness. In stressing the negative and overwhelming effects of social relations and social structures, persons are made into social 'victims', dupes and puppets, manipulated by ideology and deprived of agency.
>
> (1997: 99)

The technology of the self in critical pedagogy is one based on ideology critique, whereby the aim is to analyse and uncover one's ideological positioning, to understand how this positioning operates in the interests of oppression, and through dialogue and action free oneself of 'false consciousness'. The problem with this approach is that it theorises a self which is capable of moving from 'false' to 'true' consciousness: that is, a rational and unified self which is capable of freeing itself from its social situatedness. It is this which links critical pedagogy with the andragogical and humanistic traditions, traditions which it opposes for their individualistic approach.

Arguably in the social sciences, and the educational technologies they foster, the problematic of the social within the self is traditionally framed in terms of a binary opposition or dualism between the 'individual' and 'society'. It is as if the two poles 'individual' and 'society' are antithetical, separate, and pull in opposite directions. Moreover, theoretical positions which pose an ongoing dialectical interaction between 'individual' and 'society' have hitherto been unable to escape the dualism and invariably privilege one term over the other. For example, there have been a number of attempts in

psychology to theorise the social component of psychological functioning, particularly in social and developmental psychology. Concepts
such as 'internalisation', 'interaction', 'intersubjectivity', 'accommodation', 'shaping', 'role' and 'modelling' are recognisable as part of
the vernacular adopted by psychology to explain how the 'outside'
gets 'inside'. From a postmodern point of view, they all fail because
they are based on an acceptance of the individual-society dualism.
Theories which stress 'shaping' and 'modelling', for example, assume
a totally passive individual who is moulded by external forces.
Theories which employ the concepts of 'interaction', 'internalisation',
'accommodation', 'role' and 'intersubjectivity' ultimately rely on the
existence of a unitary, rational, pre-given individual subject.

It is of course possible to develop a way of theorising subjectivity
which is not reliant on this individual-society dualism. The concepts
of individual and society can be recast as effects which are produced
rather than as pre-given entities. For example, the idea of the unitary,
coherent and rational subject as agent can be 'deconstructed' as being
a historical product, best seen as a discourse embedded in everyday
practices and as part of the productive work of, say, psychology and
its associated educational technologies. Therefore, replacing this
view of the individual is the idea of the subject as a position within
a discourse. Moreover, because there are a number of discourses, a
number of subject positions are produced, and because discourses are
not necessarily coherent or devoid of contradiction, subjectivity is regarded as multiple, not purely rational, and potentially contradictory.
This implies a decentring of the self away from the notion of a coherent 'authentic' self and towards the notion of 'multiple subjectivities',
'multiple lifeworlds' or 'multiple layers' to everyone's identity.

To summarise, traditional theorisations of adult education practice
invariably privilege one of the two poles of the individual-society
dualism: the psychological/humanistic pole which stresses the agency
of the subject, and the sociological/critical theory pole which stresses
how the subject is wholly determined. The dilemma for the educator
is that neither pole offers a satisfactory perspective on practice: the
former seems too naive in failing to acknowledge the power of social
forces, and the latter is too pessimistic and leaves no scope for education to have a meaningful role, and there is certainly no role for the
autonomous learner. A way out of this dilemma is to deny the binary
opposition on which it is built, and treat the 'subject' and the 'social'
as jointly produced through discursive practices.

Reflection on experience as a pedagogical technology

By engaging with the above issues, educators can begin to pose questions about how they intervene to produce personal change and what their interventions reveal about their assumptions regarding the self. Do our interventions assume a false consciousness among learners? Do we assume that our interventions assist learners to overcome their social situatedness (personal history, experience of oppression etc.)? Are our interventions aimed at helping learners discover their 'real' selves? Do our interventions promote a stronger, more autonomous sense of self? Do we assume that an integrated, coherent, autonomous self is both desirable and possible? Or are our interventions aimed at exploring the multi-layered and multi-faceted nature of a purely relational self? Each one of these positions, if adopted, leads to the formulation of particular types of educational goals and the adoption of processes and ways of talking with learners which are quite different.

This can be illustrated with respect to a widely endorsed 'technology' in education: the analysis of personal and collective experiences for the purpose of learning. The traditions mentioned above (training and efficiency, andragogical, learner-centred and critical pedagogy) all have a 'version' of 'learning from experience'. And they each develop and deploy pedagogical tools which foster such learning. The general approach to learning from experience can be stated quite simply. The first task is get people to talk or write about their experiences. The second task is to analyse those experiences individually or collectively. The third task is to identify and act on the implications of what is revealed. This basic framework has spawned a number of approaches which are now well documented.

Brookfield (1991: 177), for example, regards critical reflection as the key to learning from experience and self-change. This entails three phases:

1   the identification of the assumptions that underlie thoughts and actions;
2   the scrutiny of the accuracy and validity of these assumptions in terms of how they connect to experience;
3   the reconstituting of these assumptions to make them more inclusive and integrative.

It is the recognition and analysis of assumptions which is the key to critical reflection. In the critical incident approach 'learners are asked to produce richly detailed accounts of specific events and then move to a collaborative, inductive analysis of general elements embedded in these particular descriptions' (Brookfield 1991: 181). Brookfield describes three examples of critical incident exercises he has devised. They all follow the same pattern: the participants are asked to describe a concrete event that has triggered an emotional response. They are guided in describing this event in terms of when, where and who was involved. Then follows further guidance on how to proceed, which is standardised for all three exercises:

> Now, find two other participants to form a group of three. In this triad, each person will take a turn reading aloud his or her description. After you have read out your description, your two colleagues will try to identify the assumptions about good educational practice that they think are embedded in your description. You, in turn, will do the same for each of your colleagues. To help you identify assumptions, it might be helpful to think of them as the rules of thumb that underlie and inform our actions. In this exercise, they are the general beliefs, commonsense ideas, or intuitions that you and your colleagues hold about teaching.
>
> Your analysis of assumptions should initially be on two levels: (1) What assumptions do you think inform your colleagues' choices of significant incidents – what do their choices say about their value systems? (2) What assumptions underlie the specific actions they took in the incidents described? After your description has been analysed by your two colleagues, you have the opportunity to comment on what you see as the accuracy and validity of their insights. Do you think they have gauged accurately the assumptions you hold? Were you surprised by their analyses? Or did the assumptions they identify confirm how you see your own practice? They, in turn, will have the chance to comment on the accuracy and validity of your assessments of their assumptions.
>
> It is also interesting to look for commonalities and differences in the assumptions you each identify. If there are commonly held assumptions, do they represent what passes for conventional wisdom in your field of practice? If there are major differences, to what extent might these signify divergent views in the field at large? Or might the differences be the result of contextual variations?
>
> (Brookfield 1991: 182–3)

This exercise concludes with a group analysis of assumptions. The general features of the exercise are:

- the focus is on the learners' experiences (those which are emotionally significant);
- learners work from the specific to the general;
- there is an emphasis on peer learning;
- assumptions that comprise conventional wisdom are analysed;
- there is a debriefing on the form and focus of the exercise.

In a later development of this work, Brookfield (1995: 28) regards critical reflection as 'the hunting of assumptions of power and hegemony. The best way to unearth these assumptions is to look at what we do from as many unfamiliar angles as possible'. In proposing ways of unearthing assumptions he begins by identifying 'four critically reflective lenses', one of which is autobiography. But one's autobiography is not seen as something which is open to reinterpretation and re-authoring. Instead it is seen as something which needs to be 'unearthed' so as to expose its influence on our beliefs and practices as teachers:

> Analyzing our autobiographies as learners has important implications for how we teach . . . the insights and meanings we draw from these deep experiences are likely to have a profound and long lasting influence . . . we may think we're teaching according to a widely accepted curricular or pedagogic model, only to find, on reflection, that the foundations of our practice have been laid in our autobiographies as learners.
>
> (1995: 31)

Note the emphasis here on autobiography as a foundation of practice, the uncovering of which leads to a better understanding and explanation for our otherwise uncritically accepted beliefs and commitments regarding teaching and learning. But this approach assumes a singular biography, which, however open to denial and distortion in the process of reflection, is nevertheless available to be 'discovered'. The pedagogical emphasis is therefore on the accurate rendering of one's autobiography, which invariably means addressing the distortions and denials blocking such an accurate rendition.

Thus one's biography is conceived as a lens through which the world is seen or as an internal model which guides identity and action. The role of educational intervention is to explore different ways of viewing the world and different internal models to guide action – i.e. to construct new or 'replacement' biographical narratives which are more accurate or at least more functional and adaptive for the person concerned. The resulting re-authoring of the self has as a normative goal – a single, unified and coherent narrative which resides in the mind of a single individual. Arguably this is the general conception of the self and self-change adopted by the various 'traditions' identified by Boud (1989).

This is also apparent in the plethora of teaching and training strategies and techniques documented in numerous texts supporting the skills of educators and trainers. An exemplar of such texts is *Developing Adult Learners* (Taylor *et al.* 2000), which, among other things, is an anthology of over 70 activities used by adult educators that 'attempt to draw out adults' experiences and reflections on experience as a major strategy toward learning that can lead to changes in attitudes, beliefs, understanding, and behaviors'. Each activity is separately authored and reported using a common format which includes a statement of purpose. Table 1.1 sets out a selection of purposes for each of the activities cited.

The activities prescribed to address the above purposes vary from the individual or group administration of highly structured psychological/learning instruments (e.g. the repertory grid, the Myers-Briggs Indicator, the Kolb Learning Style Inventory, the Hemispheric Preference Scale) to a more unstructured collective identification and sharing of experiences relating to a particular theme, such as blockages to one's vision, the unearthing of tacit knowledge or the bringing together of cognitive and affective modes of operating. Similar approaches are apparent in another recent volume *Challenges of Practice: Transformative Learning in Action* (Wiessner *et al.* 2000), which describes a range of strategies, techniques and programmes deployed for the purposes of transformative learning in a variety of contexts (e.g. relating to anti-racism, drug offender education, control of violence, urban reform, small businesses, workplaces, the arts, and spiritual and personal transformation).

Despite the apparent diversity, it is possible to discern in all these activities a common thread: the discovery of a deeper or truer self, the development of a more unified (strong) and coherent identity, a more integrated self – and, importantly, a self transformed through a change in the assumptions, perceptions or paradigms (i.e. the 'lens' or 'model') through which one views the world.

Table 1.1 A selection of activities used by adult educators and their purposes

Title of activity	Purpose of activity
Examining your paradigms (Proehl)	To recognize the power of paradigms in guiding thoughts and patterns, examine one's paradigms that affect attitudes and work values, and share with others one's basic assumptions or paradigms about work (p. 120)
Perspective shift (Munaker)	To introduce a strategy for an individual or members of the group to 'stand above' or outside both their rational and intuitive selves and to help a learner tap his or her tacit knowledge (p. 112)
Discovering true perceptions (Morton)	To increase awareness of one's perceptions and views of life and to assess what may be 'holding one back' (p. 110)
Symbols circle (Hicks)	To help individuals define, own, name, and claim their own experience; and to challenge the larger worldview while shoring up their own (p. 103)
Action learning (O'Neill and Marsick)	To promote development, change and transformation in individuals, teams, and organizations; help individuals learn how to learn; and solve real problems for which there is no obvious solution (p. 97)
Repertory grids (Candy)	To raise to the level of awareness a learner's assumptions as a springboard for conscious analysis of those assumptions toward greater self-understanding (p. 50)
Contradictions workshop (Dunn)	To discern and name the underlying patterns, structures and limiting beliefs in the present circumstances – that is, the contradictions, that block a group's vision – so that strategic, corrective action might be taken (p. 56)
Educational autobiographies (Clark and Kilgore)	To encourage learners to identify and reflect on specific life events, in this case, educational experiences; construct a cohesive interpretation of those experiences in an integrated way [and] critically assess their own interpretations (p. 69)
Translating personal experience into experiential essays (Eive)	To translate personal experiences into generalizations or 'universal' principles that apply to other similar problems and situations, and to discuss the results of this analysis in an experiential learning essay (p. 72)

Source: Taylor *et al.* 2000

What is problematic about this approach and what alternatives are available? Gergen and Kaye (1992: 179), writing in a therapeutic context, set out the limitations of the metaphors of the 'internal model' or 'internal lens' for understanding self-change:

for many making the postmodern turn in therapy, the narrative continues to be viewed as either a form of internal lens, determining the way in which life is seen, or an internal model for the guidance of action . . . these conceptions are found lacking in three important respects. First, each retains the *individualist* cast of modernism, in that the final resting place of the narrative construction is within the mind of the single individual . . . Secondly, the metaphors of the lens and the internal model both favor *singularity in narrative*, that is, both tend to presume the functionality of a single formulation of self understanding. The individual possesses a 'lens' for comprehending the world, it is said, not a *repository* of lenses; and through therapy one comes to possess 'a new narrative truth', it is often put, not a *multiplicity* of truths . . . Finally, both the lens and the internal model conceptions favor belief in or *commitment to narrative*. That is, both suggest that the individual lives *within* the narrative as a system of understanding . . . to be committed to a given story of self, to adopt it as 'now true for me', is vastly to limit one's possibilities of relating.

Gergen and Kaye's alternative is to see the self as relational, as a form of language game. In the exploration of new ways of relating to others, a multiplicity of self-accounts is invited, but a commitment to none. In a therapeutic context, such an approach:

encourages the client, on the one hand, to explore a variety of means of understanding the self, but discourages a commitment to any of these accounts as standing for the 'truth of self'. The narrative constructions thus remain fluid, open to the shifting tides of circumstance – to the forms of dance that provide fullest sustenance . . . The idea of the 'self' changing according to the relationship in which one is engaged illustrates a shift in focus from individual selves coming together to form a relationship, to one where the relationship takes centre stage, with selves being realized only as a by-product of relatedness. Thus it is a misconstrual to regard shifting self narratives as somehow self serving or deceitful: it is simply to recognize that each portrayal of self operates with the conventions of a particular relationship; it is 'to take seriously the multiple and varied forms of human connectedness that make up life'.

(1992: 255)

What are the implications of adopting a relational view of the self? It seems that such a view implies a certain attitude towards what critical self-reflection may achieve as a pedagogical tool. It implies for example that there is no necessity to search for an invariant or definitive story. Indeed it would be overly rigid and prescriptive to develop a singular narrative which simply replaces an earlier, more dysfunctional one, because singular narratives restrain and limit the capacity to explore different relationships. The emphasis instead is on the indeterminacy of identity, the relativity of meaning and the generation and exploration of a multiplicity of meanings. To return to Gergen and Kaye, there is a 'progression from learning new meanings, to developing new categories of meaning, to transforming one's premises about the nature of meaning itself' (1992: 257). Under what conditions can such transformations occur? Anderson and Goolishian (1992) cite the following:

- Where learners have the experience of being heard
- Where learners have their point of view and feelings understood
- Where learners feel themselves confirmed and accepted.

This involves a form of interested enquiry on behalf of the educator, one which opens premises for exploration. It also implies an openness to different ways of punctuating experience and a readiness to explore multiple perspectives and endorse their coexistence. Such interventions ostensibly enable learners to construct things from different viewpoints, releasing them from the oppression of limiting narrative beliefs. Learners can be invited to:

> find exceptions to their predominating experience; to view themselves as prisoners of a culturally inculcated story they did not create; to imagine how they might relate their experience to different people in their lives; to consider what response they might invite via their interactional proclivities; to relate what they imagine to be the experience of others close to them; to consider how they would experience their lives if they operated from different assumptions – how they might act, what resources they could call upon in different contexts; what new solutions might emerge; and to recall precepts once believed, but now jettisoned.
>
> (Anderson and Goolishian 1992: 258)

At first glance this appears to be strikingly similar to existing practices in 'critical reflection' as exemplified by Brookfield. But in Brookfield's scenario the emphasis at the outset is on discovery rather than creation: the questions posed are 'Who am I?', 'Have I got it right?' and 'What is the secret of my desire?', rather than 'Is this rendering of experience/autobiography desirable?' and 'What relationships can be invented or modulated through such a rendering of experience?' It is the latter questions which are posed when adopting a relational view of the self. Although some of the teaching techniques may be similar on the surface (e.g. exploring alternative interpretations with others), the whole project is fundamentally different. For example, in exploring one's positionality as a teacher, the task is not to 'discover' and problematise 'who we are' or 'how we are positioned' in terms of race, gender, class, sexual orientation or ableness; but to explore multiple stories around each of these categories with a view to opening up new relations of power and authority (see Tisdell 1998 for a slightly different treatment of positionality in poststructuralist feminist pedagogy). Thus from a relational point of view the pedagogy of self-reflection insists not on discovering who one is, but on creating who one might become.

Teacher-learner relationships and identity work

In any analysis of pedagogies of change, consideration of the teacher's positioning cannot be separated from that of the learners. With respect to the 'traditions' referred to earlier, there has been a general shift from 'education' to 'learning'. This has been accompanied by the increasing importance and centrality of the 'learner' as opposed to the 'teacher' in the pedagogical process. Of course the idea of learner-centredness and the changing 'teacher-learner' relationship it implies is not new. The literature in adult education, for example, has placed a great deal of emphasis on the importance of establishing an appropriate 'adult' teacher-learner relationship with the learner at the 'centre'. There has been a concern with how power should be distributed between the teacher and the learners and among learners. Who should determine when, where, how and what will be learned? What special status and privileges, if any, should be accorded the teacher? Whose interests are served by a particular kind of teacher-learner relationship? Freire's distinction between 'banking education' and 'problem posing education' and Rogers' and Knowles' ideas of the 'learning facilitator' (as opposed to the teacher) are illustrative of attempts to reconfigure the teacher-learner relationship (see Tennant and Pogson 1995).

A common thread in both critical and humanistic pedagogy is that learners are given more power and responsibility over what they learn and they are crucially seen as *producers* of knowledge, or at least as the source of knowledge. This is evident in the various activities and strategies described above and it is generally the case with learning focused on change. The 'teacher' in these circumstances can take up a number of positions: an arbiter of what constitutes worthy knowledge, a guide who assists learners to 'learn from experience', a measurement specialist who monitors performance, a facilitator who 'processes' the concerns and interests of learners, or a commentator or decoder who addresses issues of power and authority. Of course an additional complexity is that those who are learners in one context (or moment) may become teachers in another. In many instances teachers of adults are the subordinates of their learners in the larger organisational or professional context. For example, this role flexibility, and even ambiguity is a feature of most workplace learning situations where there is a need to manage personal change in line with broader organisational change.

The teacher-learner relationship in pedagogies of change is clearly one which is shifting and constantly open to negotiation. In this scenario learners seem to be empowered in the sense that they are enjoined to be active subjects. But the accompanying self-regulation and surveillance is arguably disempowering: learners being co-opted (or perhaps 'duped') into managing themselves in line with both organisational and educational requirements. In these circumstances the real skill of the learners is to find spaces for 'self-creation' among the contested meanings of experience bound to emerge from the different perspectives of the employer, teacher and learner. Thus the learner needs to be able to critique the discourse of experiential learning while paradoxically adopting this discourse – i.e. to maintain a sceptical and questioning attitude to the various ways in which they are positioned and experience is reconstituted as learning. A corresponding role for the teacher is to adopt the discourse of experiential learning while simultaneously engaging in a critique of this discourse with the learners. In this way there is an ongoing co-construction of new teacher-learner relationships, in effect pre-empting 'closure' on any fixed teacher identity such as 'expert', 'guide' or 'facilitator'.

We should emphasise here that many facets of contemporary educational practice and theorising have a bearing on teacher-learner identities: the decentring of the teacher, learners reflecting on and deconstructing their experiences, the exploration of alternative readings of experience, the contested nature of knowledge, greater learner control of the processes and aims of learning, the breakdown of the teacher-learner dichotomy, more open-ended curricula and pedagogical practices, the recognition of the power of discourse to shape people's lives, the recognition of diversity among students, the challenging of disciplinary knowledge and the acknowledgment that knowledge is generated through experiences at work, in the family and in community life. It is also evident that the boundaries between the sectors of education are breaking down, particularly between formal and non-formal education and between education delivered at different sites and locations. There is no doubt that what constitutes knowledge is being contested and reframed by our educational institutions. In this context it is clear that issues of identity are not isolated to those programmes which have an explicit change agenda.

Concluding comments

Accepting that education invariably involves an element of self-formation and change, very different 'selves' can be found in various pedagogical practices and theories. This has been illustrated in this chapter in three ways. First, through pointing to how different pedagogical traditions can be located as emphasising one or the other terms in the dualism of 'individual' and 'society': the training and efficiency tradition, the self-direction or andragogical tradition, the learner-centred or humanistic tradition and the critical pedagogy and social action tradition. Second, through examining a particular pedagogical tool: reflection on experience as a means of personal change. And finally through looking at the way in which teacher-learner relationships and identity work are linked to the adoption of particular pedagogical practices.

This chapter has mainly focused on a discussion of the self in educational terms. In doing so it has made use of the terms 'self', 'subjectivity' and 'identity'. The following chapter explains the theoretical context in which these terms have emerged, analyses the increasing interest in identity, and draws attention to a discursive and social approach to identity formation.

Chapter 2

Theorising identity

Introduction

Our aim in this book is to examine how and in what ways pedagogical strategies work to change learner identities. However, in order to proceed we need to make more explicit what we mean when we speak of identity, for this is a contested concept subject to ongoing dispute. In this chapter we outline what identity means to us and provide an overview of the different meanings that continue to be ascribed to the concept.

In the previous chapter we drew attention to the way all education and training programmes, irrespective of rationale, invariably imply change of some sort. Furthermore we argued that these programmes also suggest at least an element of self-transformation for participants involved in the experience. Learners, either explicitly or implicitly, are thought to emerge from the learning experience different in some way from when they entered. They emerge more 'knowledgeable', 'skilled', 'motivated', 'assertive', 'creative' or 'critical', depending on the particular aim (and success) of the programme.

But who is this 'self' that is being transformed? What kind of subjectivity is being changed? What kind of learning identity is being (re)constructed? Indeed, what do concepts such as the 'self', the 'subject' and 'identity' mean today in terms of our understanding of 'self'? These are the questions explored in this chapter.

Self, subjectivity and identity

In the human and social sciences, terms such as the 'self', the 'subject' and 'subjectivity' have recently been the focus of unprecedented critique. The tendency of these categories to represent the 'self' as a unified and integral construct, at the centre of the self-sustaining individual, has been problematised, as have notions of the 'self' that constitute it as the product of social relations. Increasingly, discourses to do with ideas of the 'self' use terms such as 'contingency', 'multiplicity' and 'fragmentation', and the term 'identity' in particular has come to the fore in contemporary discourses that speak of subjectivity.

The reasons for this discursive shift involve, among other things, the assertion that concepts of the 'self' should not be seen as neutral representations of the subject-person but rather as discursive interventions that do important political and cultural work in constructing, maintaining and transforming both individuals and their social world. Contemporary feminist, postcolonial and cultural studies commentators have, for example, pointed to the way in which conceptions of identity based on notions of gender, class, race and national or cultural allegiance, work to obliterate difference through the discursive construction of sameness (Pateman 1989; hooks 1990; Butler 1993). Others highlight the fragility and constructed nature of identity, arguing that it has no enduring meaning but is subject to continuing cultural and historical reformation (Hall and du Gay 1996). While commentators such as Rosaldo (1993) point to the immanent connection between identity and cultural formation.

Much of this critique distances itself from a concept of identity that posits the self as a unified and essential core at the centre of subjectivity. Rather, the self is configured as a contingent and constructed concept, one that is subject to continuing social and historical transformation. This critique also rejects a conception of identity based on the recognition of some naturally occurring set of similarities, common characteristics or shared understandings that characterise particular individuals or social groupings at particular historical moments. Moreover, the term has come to mean a process rather than a product; a process that involves a construction of sameness that is continually evolving and incomplete. Furthermore, because identification is a process that imposes itself across difference, it is also a process that requires discursive work in order to construct the symbolic boundaries used to differentiate one particular identification from that which surrounds it. In other words, without discursive work the process of identification across difference is impossible.

This discursive approach to identity formation has a number of implications. First, it suggests that identities are never unified but consist of multiple processes of identification that are constructed by different, often intersecting and sometimes antagonistic, discursive practices that make particular identifications possible. This leads to the idea that the formation of identity cannot be justified on the grounds that it merely reflects pre-existing patterns of sameness, but rather owes its existence to particular discursive interventions. This in turn suggests that identity formation is both a strategic and context-bound process. Identities are constructed through the deployment of specific enunciative strategies and are produced in specific institutional sites at particular historical moments.

In this chapter we look at the different ways in which the concept of identity is understood. We begin by suggesting that the current interest in identity is in many ways the result of a much broader critique of the ideas and practices associated with modernity.

Identities in crisis

Recently, in the human and social sciences, there has been an explosion of interest in the notion of identity. At the same time, and somewhat paradoxically, the concept has been the subject of unprecedented critique. Some contemporary commentators reject the concept entirely, suggesting that identity is a modern fiction (Rorty 1989) or an invention of modernity (Bauman 1996). Others propose that the current deep ambivalence towards the notion of identity opens up the possibility for individuals to create new and imaginative representations of the self (Elliott 1996). Commentators such as Giddens (1991, 1994) and Beck (1992; Beck *et al.* 1994) reconfigure identity in terms of a reflexive rewriting of the self, made possible by the continuous self-monitoring processes that characterise late modernity. While Hall (Hall and du Gay 1996) calls for a radical reconceptualisation of the concept, one that recognises the complex relationship between identity formation and discourse.

These commentaries are in many ways constructed on the back of a much wider critique of modernity that has questioned almost all of the philosophical, epistemological, social and cultural assumptions that have underpinned dominant understandings of the modern world. Various commentators have pointed to the inadequacies and ambiguities prevalent in many of the ideas and assumptions that characterise modernity. Some have initiated a political critique of the modern state (e.g. Hall and Jaques 1989; Perryman 1994), while others have problematised the traditional sociological assumptions used to explain modern social formations (Wagner 1994). Feminist writers have critiqued modernity in terms of its gendered construction, its privileging of 'rational thought' and its foundational epistemology (Lloyd 1984; Luke and Gore 1992; Hekman 1994), and postcolonial writers have critiqued modernity in terms of its Eurocentrism (Bhabha

1992). Postmodern commentators have launched critiques of the modernist conception of reality (Baudrillard 1989), its assumption of progress (Deleuze 1983; Vattimo 1988), its truth claims (Rorty 1989) and its conception of knowledge (Lyotard 1984).

While recognising the disparate nature of these discourses, what they all display is a scepticism towards many of the assumptions that have underpinned modernity's understanding of itself. These discourses suggest that western culture, with its feet firmly planted in Enlightenment rationalism, is based on the belief that everything can or will be explained. Faced with increasingly complex sets of economic, social, cultural and political problems that continue to defy resolution, the western cultural tradition is caught in crisis, increasingly aware of the inadequacy of these explanations in providing some certainty to human action.

By undermining many of the assumptions and understandings that have guided modern thinking, these commentaries have, as the work of Rorty (1989), Bauman (1996), Elliot (1996), Giddens (1994), du Gay (1996a) and others illustrates, also problematised conceptions of identity that are grounded within the ideas and assumptions of modernity. In this chapter, we explore the various theorisations of identity formation in order to situate them within the ideas and assumptions that have characterised modernity. We suggest that these theorisations need not be seen as enduring, transcendental constructions but rather as socially and historically located concepts, intimately connected to the changing face of modernity. Furthermore, we propose that their changing nature need not be seen as the result of some gradual refinement of our understanding of identity. Rather, they can be seen as concepts that do specific kinds of work by shaping particular understandings and social practices, and bringing new social practices into play. All of these concepts continue to have effects on our understanding of the process of identity formation.

Bauman writes that identity 'is an invention of modernity' (see Hall and du Gay 1996: 18). The assertion made here is that identity has also been subject to numerous reinventions, all of which continue to have effects on contemporary constructions of identity.

The meaning of modernity

Before embarking on an analysis of the ways in which the various concepts of identity are inscribed within the various historical, social and cultural change processes that mark modernity, our definition of 'modernity' needs some explanation. Our account is by no means a definitive description of modernity – rather, it sets out those features that have in some ways shaped contemporary understandings of identity.

Modernity is itself a complex concept. As Bradbury and McFarlane (1976: 22) point out, within normal usage, the modern is seen as something that progresses in company with, and at the speed of, the years – like the bow-wave of a ship; last year's modern is not this year's. The modern is therefore *always* in formation. It represents the 'transient, the fleeting, the contingent'[1] (Baudelaire in Harvey 1990: 10). Inevitably, once formed, it loses its title to the *next* historical moment.

This common-sense meaning of the term becomes problematic when social and cultural commentators attempt to assign the modern a place in history; for in order to identify the modern, a description of it must be developed. The meaning of the modern therefore shifts from being *anything* of the here and now to being identified as a set of underlying assumptions and common characteristics that stamp a particular socio-cultural process or product as 'modern'. Individuals, institutions, cultural processes and products that reveal some or all of these characteristics are described as 'modern'. Modernity achieves a trans-historical dimension, linking different examples of itself across historical periods. It also offers a trans-spatial dimension, linking examples of itself across continents, and also achieves a trans-disciplinary dimension, offering a meta-theory that encompasses the various disciplines found within the western intellectual tradition. Thus, modernity comes to represent particular ways of thinking and acting in the world that are underpinned by a set of common assumptions and suppositions.

Commentators have tackled the issue of modernity from a number of positions. Habermas (1985) traces the origins of modernity in terms of the philosophical ideas that are associated with the concept. Foucault (1977) examines the rise of modern knowledge and the self-disciplining subject. Wagner (1994) looks to the sociological constructions that are formed in modernity. Harvey (1990) writes about the cultural change processes embedded in modernity, and Perryman (1994) looks to the political and economic discourses that are associated with modernity.

Despite the different concerns of these commentators, they all appear to associate modernity in one way or another with changes that occurred in western Europe from the late sixteenth century onwards. Commonly, these changes are seen as coming out of three related historical occurrences:

- the emergence of scientific rationality as a key approach to knowledge creation;
- the emergence of social pluralism as a result of the Industrial Revolution and the adoption of mass production;
- the emergence of the liberal democratic state as the political personification of modernity.

There are dangers in making these broad generalisations, as these occurrences can be viewed as particular historical events that revolutionised western societies. The economic, social and political changes surrounding these events were slow and uneven, in terms of their temporal, spatial and social distribution, and while they signalled the emergence of new concepts, ideas and discursive practices, these new ways of interpreting the world were still only of interest to very small minorities in these changing societies. However, while recognising these dangers, there can be little doubt that the new ideas and ways of thinking that emerged have had important implications for the construction of modern concepts of identity.

In the next three sections we turn to the concepts of identity that have emerged in modernity. We recognise that this account cannot do full justice to this complex topic, however we make the claim that this account is useful in terms of understanding how the various concepts of identity are shaped by the various discourses of modernity. Our aim is to trace the effects of these different constructions on contemporary concepts of identity.

We suggest that three theoretical schema underpin modern conceptions of identity. The first involves positing a knowing conscious subject at the centre of individual identity and is arguably the earliest invention of the modern subject. The second invokes the power of social relations in identity formation. The clash between these two theoretical positions dominated debates in the human and social sciences for most of the twentieth century and has been resolved, at least in the minds of some, by positing identity as the dialectic outcome of the interaction between the essential self and social relations.

We propose that the third, and most recent, theoretical schema points to the power of language and discourse in the construction of identity and is a significant departure from previous debates over identity. This does not aim to supplant previous concepts of identity with newer and 'truer' ones, but rather attempts to surface the work done by different concepts of identity in constructing particular understandings of the self. Further, it points to the pivotal role identity plays in the politics of location, be it based on nationality, ethnic origin, gender, class, race, sexuality or occupation. At the same time, it also reveals the difficulties that characterise all forms of 'identity politics' that are based on privileging particular identities over others. This discursive approach also sees the construction of identity as an ambiguous process that is always unstable, multiple and in formation. An example of this discursive approach to identity formation is explored further in Chapter 3.

Identity and scientific rationality

The antecedents of scientific rationality can, according to Habermas (1985: 16), be traced to the 'discovery' of the 'New World', the Renaissance and the Reformation in Europe. These events signalled a renewed interest in the external material world of nature and a concomitant indifference to the internal spiritual world dominated by the Church. In the seventeenth century the work of Galileo and Newton epitomised this change and began what has come to be known as the Age of Enlightenment in Europe. Galileo and Newton undermined the spiritually governed world of Europe by positing science as the primary investigative tool required to understand the real material world of nature. Through science 'Man'[2] was seen as being capable of determining a set of absolute rules that interacted with each other in predetermined, predictable ways and thereby was capable of understanding and controlling the material world of nature.

These explanations of the world were a radical departure from theistic explanations of both the world and the human condition. In Europe, theistic determinism held that God was all knowing, controlling the world and all living things in the world. The conclusions of Galileo and the work of Newton questioned this orthodoxy and initiated a challenge to theistic determinism. 'Man' ceased being a creature of God in seventeenth-century Europe and emerged as a creature of 'Man', capable of understanding and controlling the material world of nature. The discursive shift from God to 'Man' can clearly be seen in the writings of Pierre Laplace (1749–1827), when discussing the possibilities of Newtonian science:

such an intelligence could embrace in the same formula the movements of the greatest bodies of the universe and those of the
lightest atom: for it nothing would be uncertain and the future as
the past, would be present to its eyes.

(Gleick 1988: 14)

The French philosopher Descartes (1596–1650) linked human reason to the project of science in order to achieve certainty of knowledge. Descartes rejected the philosophy based on Aristotelian logic
that accepted the eternal and qualitative differences that characterised the classification of the things of the world. Descartes' interest
was to discover unifying theories that overcame these supposed eternal differences. He regarded these differences with suspicion because
they were the antecedents of doubt, and as Burbules (1995: 4) argues
Cartesian doubt was: 'a doubt which says that whatever is not clear
and certain must be rejected as foundational. Cartesian doubt was
always doubt in the service of seeking certainty'. Thus Descartes
began a systematic search for universal truth and certainty using the
analytical methods borrowed from mathematics to analyse the world
of thought. He looked for generalisable truths that would deliver the
platform on which certainty could be grounded. This rationalist thesis
argued that though knowledge could be gained by human beings in a
number of ways, including via the imaginative and emotional spheres,
knowledge gained by way of reason was superior in terms of progress
to human understanding. Human problems could best be solved by
way of the rigorous application of logic to proven facts. Rationalism
thus entered the discursive world of modernity, with its promise of
finding generalisable and universal truths that would provide certainty in an uncertain world.

Other philosophers such as Bacon, Locke and Hume continued the
theorisation of science by attempting to rid philosophy of two uncertainties. The first was the recognition of the fallibility of the human
mind set against the need to rely on hypotheses generated by that
same mind to establish the truth of the material world. The second
was the acknowledged limited and limiting capacity of the human
senses to identify and recognise the complex and often hidden elements making up the material world.

These philosophers attempted to overcome these philosophical
imperfections by developing foundational and objective 'laws of
science' that governed the external world of matter. Based on the
exact sciences of mathematics and physics, tied to the rigorous

experimental research of natural phenomena, they explained the world through empirical analysis. Thus empiricism joined rationalism as the key characteristic of western science and science itself became a dominating feature of the Enlightenment; with claims that science and science alone could provide certain knowledge and material progress.

It can be argued that scientific rationality constructs the subject-person in a particular way. The rational knowing, conscious subject becomes the privileged identity of the Enlightenment. The German philosopher Hegel makes this clear when providing a philosophical description of the modern 'subject'. He emphasises individualism as the defining characteristic of the modern subject and also adds, as necessary prerequisites to identity formation, the right of subjects to individual freedom and autonomous action (Habermas 1985: 16–17).

Scientific rationality constructs the modern subject as an active individual human agent, capable of employing logical thought to investigate the world in order to find the universal rules that govern it. *Agency* – i.e. the ability to act in the world – becomes a central feature of individual identity and is closely related to the concept of individual *autonomy*. The autonomous individual is in the best position to explore the material world of nature.

However, Cartesian *rationality* also effectively constrains individual agency and autonomy. The individual subject can discover the universal truths of existence and insert certainty into the world *only* through the act of rational thought. The aesthetic, imaginative and sensual domains of human understanding become suspect in Cartesian rationalism. It rejects other ways of coming to know the world, regarding them as inferior to rationality. Thus, while rationality is discursively framed as the privileged way of coming to know the world, at the same time it also acts as a constraint over individual agency. Freedom to act is not total but is constrained by being governed by a particular way of thinking.

Empirical method also, albeit in a different way, constrains notions of agency and autonomous action by its insistence that investigations must follow the tenets of scientific method. It also reinforces the immanent commitment to *individualism* in the Enlightenment construct of identity. Empirical 'Man' is seen as a pre-constituted rational individual, capable of coming to understand the external reality of the world by using empirical method.

Individuality is also emphasised by empiricism through its insistence that 'objectivity' is an essential element of scientific investigation.

The individual, though part of the world, must also be at the same time separate from the world, capable of being an objective 'outsider', using the strictures of scientific method to solve the problems of human existence. Thus individual identity is constructed as being both outside the material world of nature *and* outside the world of social relations.

Scientific rationalism was the subject of considerable critique in the twentieth century, not least by science itself. The reductionism implicit in scientific method was criticised (Birke and Silvertown 1984), while Heisenberg's uncertainty principle, Einstein's theory of relativity, the indeterminacy built into quantum physics and the conclusions of chaos theory all, in different ways, undermined many of the assumptions of scientific rationalism.

However, despite the concerted assaults on the tenets of scientific rationality within and outside of science, the conception of identity constructed by scientific rationality, to borrow the words of Habermas (1985: 24), 'continues to exercise a broad and deep, often subterranean influence' on contemporary conceptions of identity.

The rational subject acting in the world, while at the same time standing outside of the world in order to know it, remains a powerful identity figure of modernity. The 'I' in the often quoted Cartesian aphorism 'I think therefore I am' is this constructed Enlightenment identity; a conscious knowing subject, capable of purposeful action, able to control the external natural world and assert autonomy over it. This 'I' is also discursively constructed as an individual, capable of seeing the world from the privileged position of rationality. It is also framed as an exclusive 'I' – only those individuals capable of accessing the world of scientific rationality can contribute to the accumulation of useful knowledge.

The knowing conscious subject of the Enlightenment is therefore predicated on a number of a priori assumptions. The self is a rational individual. The self experiences reality in a transparent, unmediated way. 'Reality' is an independently existing given. However, these assumptions have all been the subject of critique.

Freud, for example, has highlighted the importance of the subconscious in the formation of identity. Lacan (1968) has stressed the role of language in the construction of the self. Feminist writers, such as Lloyd (1984), have pointed to the gendered nature of Enlightenment discourses. While accepting the critique of Enlightenment dualisms proposed by Derrida (1978), she argued that these dualisms (rational v. irrational, objective v. subjective, reason v. emotion etc.)

are always asymmetric and gendered within the discourses of modernity. The Enlightenment subject is discursively framed as 'Man' and becomes associated with rationality, objectivity and reason. And, by their absence within these discourses, women are discursively constructed as the 'other' of the Enlightenment, associated with irrationality, subjectivity and unreason (Hekman 1994: 50–5). Postcolonial writers have highlighted the Eurocentric nature of Enlightenment thought and the deep ambiguity engendered between colonial expansion and the discourses of emancipation and individualism at the heart of modernity's concept of identity (Bhabha 1996: 199–211).

While these contemporary critiques of the Enlightenment subject can be seen as reflecting the advantage of hindsight, there is evidence that it was the subject of some ambiguity from the time it first appeared. Locke (1632–1704) for example, while retaining the notion of the individual self (i.e. an essential identity distinguishable from others) as being constituted by the power of rational thought, also recognised the power of social relations in the formation of identity:

> no man escapes the punishment of their censure and dislike, who offends against the fashion and opinion of the company he keeps, and would recommend himself to. Nor is there one of ten thousand who is stiff and insensible enough to bear up under the constant dislike and condemnation of his own club.
>
> ([1690] 1959: 449)

For Locke, the autonomous 'I' of the Enlightenment identity was also, within the lifeworld of social relations, a socially constructed 'me'. Locke concludes therefore that individual identity is inevitably a social identity and provides one of the earliest dialectical theories of identity formation, pointing to the importance of the social world in the construction of individual identity.

Identity and social relations

The early recognition by Locke of the power of social relations in the construction of identity had particular significance in the emerging world of modernity. The social transformations that accompanied industrialisation and mass production, including urbanisation, the acceleration of the division of labour, increasing social pluralism and the emergence of the modern state, placed considerable pressure on the concept of identity embedded within the Enlightenment subject.

The identity figure of the Enlightenment was from the outset a concept that restricted itself to a small minority of individuals within society. The libertarian rhetoric concerning individual freedom and autonomy was in practice restricted to the 'bourgeois economic' and 'intellectual elites', and as Wagner (1994: 58) comments: 'the social identity of the members of these groups was shaped by their belief that they belonged to the progressive forces of society, those who would advance mankind from its often enough miserable fate'. This Enlightenment identity provided the bourgeoisie with the justification for their social and economic conduct. It was, however, an exclusive and exclusionary identity, increasingly incompatible with the complex social transformations occurring in the modern state. The economics of industrial mass production, political pressures for universal suffrage and the emergence of the democratic state created new social groupings, based on notions of collective identity, including class, national identity and political allegiance.

Social theory responded by entering a period of what some called 'grand critiques' (Wagner 1994: 62). Theorisations concerning identity moved from foundational notions of individuality to a view that the macro-social structures emerging in modernity were now the primary agents in the construction of individual identity. Two of these 'grand critiques' in particular played crucial roles in developing theories of identity formation and provide clear evidence of this change of focus in social theory. The first, the critique of political economy, developed mainly through the work of Marx and posited economic relations as the prime determinant of social formation. The second, developed by Weber, involved a political critique of modern state institutions and the rise of bureaucratic rationality within them.

Both critiques, in different ways, moved away from the idea that the individual was the centre of self-formation and focused on theorising the ways in which the macro-social structures of modernity construct people's sense of who they are. The human subject is theorised within these critiques as the product of social relations, which in turn are largely determined by the macro-social structures of the modern economy and polity. These critiques also suggest that social structures are contingent – i.e. the product of history. As Mead commented: 'We can speak of individual identity only in terms of what Marx calls the "ensemble" of social relations, whose historicity is a fundamental aspect of existence' (quoted in Aronowitz 1994: 196–7).

While Marxist theory emphasised the economic as the fundamental category of social relations, Weber's interest was in theorising the political relations that emerged in modernity, in particular the bureaucratisation processes that appeared as a fundamental characteristic in the governance of modern society. The move to universal suffrage and the consequent increased pressure for state interventions in the governance of social life led to the formation of state apparatuses, big industrial enterprises and mass parties. These macro-social structures, characterised by internal stratification, hierarchical chains of command and abstract rules of action, were identified by Weber as taking on the Enlightenment mantle of rational action. They became the sites where social progress could be assured, where competing claims could be arbitrated, where objectivity could be maintained and truth guaranteed. The rational individuality of the Enlightenment could not be extended to every citizen of the emergent modern state but needed to be appropriated within the governing social structures of society.

Weber, while recognising the progressive nature of the democratic principles implicit in the rise of the modern state, was also deeply suspicious of the ways in which these principles were implemented. He regarded the bureaucratisation process as subjecting individuals to the dominance of an instrumental rationality. Bureaucratisation builds an 'iron cage' (Aronowitz 1994: 64) based on an instrumental means-ends theory of action, that progressively controls an individual's whole existence. The individual subject is confronted by a rationality, external to itself, based on abstract and 'objective' rules of action that appear in direct contradiction to the everyday experiences of the individual's immediate lifeworld. For Weber, therefore, the modern state's governing instrumentalities work to appropriate and deny the individual's sense of who they are in modern societies.

While Weber's critique of modernity focused on political structures and their operation within social life, Marx's critique of political economy privileged economic relations in the construction of society and has, arguably, been one of the most important contributions to contemporary theorisations of identity. For Marx, the explanation for all social relations lay in the mode of production that particular societies adopted. The idea of 'economic man' was foregrounded in the Marxist theory of identity and in particular in the notion of 'alienation' in work that Marx suggested was the inevitable outcome of the capitalist mode of production.

The foregrounding of the economic structures of society together with the Marxist notion of 'alienation' continue to have a profound influence on theories that attempt to explain social and individual formation.

Identity and discourse

The focus on the power of social relations in the construction of identity often involved theorising identity in terms of the impact of the structural conditions that constituted modern societies. It commonly conceptualised identity as the product of these social structures. The Durkheimian thesis of organic solidarity and the functional division of labour, Marx's theorisation of class and its emancipatory potential and Weber's notion of the rise of rationality in state institutions all reflect an increased preoccupation with the ways in which macro-social structures determine the formation of individual identity.

All these theorisations moved away from early Enlightenment theories of identity, based on the ideas of individual rationality, agency and autonomous action, and conflated self-formation with structural issues to do with economic and social formation. Individuals were now constructed in terms of class, institutional location or shared value systems. Collective responsibility replaced individual agency in these new theorisations and identity became the product of the structural arrangements that constituted modern societies.

However, the recognition of the power of social relations in the construction of selfhood also led a number of theorists to focus on communication and language as key elements in the construction of identity. Mead was the first, but by no means the only, social theorist to point to the importance of language in the construction of the self through the processes of social interaction. Habermas also foregrounded the importance of communicative action in the creation of an intersubjective rationality to counter the excesses of Cartesian rationality, which he argued 'elevates something finite to the status of the absolute' (1985: 24). Lacan (1968) also conceptualised subjectivity as being structured: 'according to the laws of the Imaginary (the order of identifications and images) and the Symbolic (the order of language and culture)' (quoted in Usher and Edwards 1994: 62). Similarly, various feminist, postcolonial, philosophical and postmodern positions, while often presenting contradictory and occasionally antagonistic descriptions of identity formation, all implicate language as crucial in the construction of identity.

This 'linguistic turn' not only problematises the concept of identity embedded in the idea of 'Enlightenment Man' but also questions all social theories that privilege economic, social and political structures as the major determinants in the formation of identity. It does not reject the notion of social power but rather emphasises the power of language in the construction of identity. It suggests that the words and ideas that inhabit the social world cannot be seen as neutral representations of a pre-existing reality, but act as powerful practices that 'do work' by constructing particular realities. This perspective therefore locates the texts we read as being: 'a part of the social world, human life and the historical moments in which they are located and interpreted' (Said quoted in Lather 1991: 4). Power resides in all discourses including those economic, social and political theories that attempt to explain identity. Put simply, our conception of who we are, our identity, is constituted by the power of all of the discursive practices in which we speak and which in turn 'speak' us.

This poststructural perspective brings together a number of theoretical positions that are pertinent in any discussion of identity. The indeterminate, ambiguous and relational nature of words, highlighted by Derrida (1978), suggests that language cannot be seen as carrying definitive meaning or as representing any pre-existing reality. Rather, words act as exclusionary devices, their meaning being as much determined by what they leave out as what they purport to describe. Poststructuralism has also incorporated the Foucauldian idea of power (Foucault 1980, 1983). Here power is seen as immanent not only in the language that circulates in social groups, but in the very nature of knowledge. For Foucault, knowledge is itself both the product and instrument of power. Discourses are powerful because they construct particular 'regimes of truth', creating disciplinary practices that become internalised within the social subject. In Foucauldian terms, discourses are particular technologies of power that act as: 'an inspecting gaze, a gaze which each individual under its weight will end by internalising to the point that he is his own supervisor, each individual thus exercising this surveillance over, and against, himself' (Miller 1993: 223).

For Foucault, therefore, discourses are not merely technologies of power but processes of governing which align individual conduct with socio-economic objectives. So, for example, the teaching and learning strategies outlined in the case studies in Chapters 4–9, seen in this light, can be understood as pedagogical interventions that serve the objectives of particular programmes of 'governmentality'.

Therefore, we could understand the teaching and learning strategies in each of the case studies as being in one way or another technologies for producing productive global citizens. These citizens, for example, need to be self-actualising and goal setting (Chapter 4), they need to be both workers and learners (literally at the same time) and thus more productive at work (Chapter 5), they need to have safe sex and therefore remain healthy (Chapter 7) – and if they do so they will self-regulate to the goals of the programme.

One of the attractions of Foucault's notion of governmentality (1991) is that it understands the governing of the population to include programmes of the state (i.e. of Government with an upper case 'G') as well as those beyond the state (i.e. government with a lower case 'g'). This concept allows for a concern with governing not as 'the state' but as:

> all endeavours to shape, guide, direct the conduct of others, whether these be the crew of a ship, the members of a household, the employees of a boss, the children of a family or the inhabitants of a territory . . . [and] . . . embraces the ways to govern ourselves.
> (Rose 1999)

Another 'seductive' aspect of governmentality is its explanation of the productive power of the individual through the notion of 'technologies of self'. This refers to the self-steering mechanisms involved in the ways in which individuals experience, understand, judge and conduct themselves (Foucault 1986; Gordon 1991; Miller and Rose 1993; Dean and Hindess 1998; Rose 1996). This way of understanding the relationship of power and self can explain how the construction of subjects (the formation of identities) comes through participating in, and self-regulating to, programmes of government, as people make their 'own' way along trajectories, locating themselves in contemporary governmentality and all the ambiguous implications of that state.

From these perspectives, discourses act as powerful practices that do not merely construct identities but also hide their presence in the construction. These discursive practices privilege who can speak, what can be thought and said and what identity is given status at particular historical moments. Discourses become the absent presence in the construction of identity, points of governance over the actions of individuals within their lifeworld.

However, while discourses can and do operate as disciplining practices that constrain subjects they also provide the conditions of possibility for the emergence of new subjectivities. Following Foucault, explicating the tensions between the constraining and enabling effects of discursive power remains the central problematic of poststructural theories. Power is not forceful, coercive or top-down, but only powerful when the concerns of individuals are connected to macro-level interests and when power is addressed to individuals who are free to act one way or another. Therefore, while power is omnipresent, 'power in a society is never a fixed or closed regime, but rather an endless and open strategic game' (Gordon 1991: 5). This openness suggests a freedom to act which generates a counter-politics, where the terms of the practices of governmentality can be turned around into focuses of resistance. This highlights the complexities around self-regulation (i.e. the intersection of technologies of power and technologies of self), and the significance of acts of resistance in governing.

Nevertheless, there are dangers in using this discursive approach when theorising identity. First, it is possible to overemphasise either the constraining or enabling effects of discursive power in identity formation. Second, discursive explanations of identity formation can slide into a kind of discursive determinism. However, these dangers can be minimised by recognising that individuals exist in multiple discourses, simultaneously. This multiplicity means that different discourses clash, compete and interact with each other, opening up the possibility of the emergence of new understandings, knowledges, interpretations and points of resistance in the construction of selfhood. Furthermore, the ambiguous, open and duplicitous nature of language prevents any final closure of meaning. Words are continually interpreted and reinterpreted by individuals when engaged in making meaning of their lifeworld. Consequently, discursive meaning is always contingent and contextual. Finally, when new discourses enter the lifeworlds of individuals, they enter a field of already circulating discourses that often act as foci of compliance or resistance to these new discourses.

Poststructural theories emphasise the problematic nature of discourses in terms of their power to constrain and enable the construction of particular ways of being in the world. We live in a circulating world of discourses and we are required to interpret this discursive world. Yet discourses often remain unexamined in terms of the work that they perform in the construction of our identities. Poststructural theories therefore alert us to the 'lack of innocence' (Grosz 1989: xv) of discourses, through their claim to definitive knowledge and the constitutive effects they have on our understanding of our identity.

Notes

1 It is worth noting here that the description of the modern suggested by Baudelaire is in fact much closer to the contemporary discourses of postmodernity. The terms 'transient', 'fleeting' and 'contingent' sit much more comfortably within postmodern discourses than they do within the discourses of modernity.

2 The use of 'Man' here and throughout this chapter is deliberate. As Hekman (1994: 53) clearly indicates when she writes 'Although men would have us believe that the term "man" is generic, that is, that it includes the experience of both men and women, a simple example proves this false: the statement "man has difficulty in childbirth" is nonsense'. We use the word 'Man' in this chapter to indicate the gendered nature of modernity and do not subscribe to the notion that the word 'Man' is a generic term.

Chapter 3

Understanding identity as narrative

Introduction

Around the time of writing this book one of us was talking with a friend who was telling the story of a meeting he had with a high-school principal. This person had, some years ago, moved to a new city and he and his wife were going through the process of choosing a high school for their teenage son. As part of the process they met with the principals of a number of schools to help decide which one they would select. In one particular school, he asked the principal a simple question: 'How would you describe your teaching and learning approach?' In hearing the question, the principal looked back with a somewhat puzzled expression on his face and said: 'We teach and they learn.'

This simple statement – 'we teach and they learn' – although largely discredited and discarded by most contemporary educators, is interesting in that, despite it being only five words, it contains all the characteristics of a narrative. As discussed in Chapter 1, this particular narrative is not one that all strands of adult and organisational educators share, and the cases we discuss in our later chapters are, on the surface, constructed around very different narratives of pedagogy – we will return to this point later in the chapter. The statement 'we teach and they learn' is a narrative in that it sequences and emplots events over time, and this emplotment constructs a causality between those events. It defines characters (teachers and students) and implicates them in the emplotment. It has a theme that emerges through the plot (i.e. the roles of different people in the learning process). This story also works to define identity – it suggests that, in describing a teaching and learning approach, people can be classified into two types: teachers and students. Further, it is implied that those people who fall within each of these categories have different and mutually exclusive positions in the teaching and learning process. This reflects a traditional and conservative pedagogical approach that positions the teachers as the knowers whose task it is to pass knowledge on to those they teach. In turn, this positions those who assume the identities of teacher and student in a hierarchy – where, of course, the teacher is the one who is superior and hence more powerful. While the case studies in the following chapters are not about pedagogies which overtly take this form, part of the point of this book is that we are trying to show how elements of this view are nevertheless embedded within contemporary pedagogical practices.

This simple example highlights the issue that we wish to explore in this chapter: the way that narratives embody discursive power to construct particular identities within a pedagogical context. In doing so we use narratives to explore some of the ideas discussed in Chapter 2 in relation to taking on a discursive approach to identity formation. Introducing the concept of narrative enables a discussion of identity that focuses on issues of relational power and identity politics in relation to pedagogy. This cultural politics of identity in turn leads to questions that we believe are important in understanding different pedagogies – for example, what identities are presupposed in particular pedagogical practices? Which identities are constructed as dominant? Which are suppressed? In what ways does pedagogy support or limit diversity? While these questions are addressed both directly and indirectly in the case studies that follow, our purpose here is to discuss how a narrative perspective on identity enables these questions to be brought to the fore and productively discussed.

Whereas Chapter 1 focused on how forms of the 'relational self' are embedded in pedagogy, and Chapter 2 examined the theoretical background of the notion of identity and self, here our attention turns to a more detailed examination of the discursive *processes* through which identity is informed. We do this by drawing on and developing a theoretical perspective based on the relationship between narrative and identity. Our intent in highlighting the notion of narrative identity in this book is a pragmatic one – we are less interested in making claims to the 'truth' of a narrative perspective and more interested in how such a perspective can be productively used.

In exploring narrative and identity, this chapter proceeds in three parts. We start by putting forward a particular view on the relationship between narrative and identity. Here we distinguish between two interdependent processes of narrative identity formation: *reflexive identification* (which sees identity in terms of a person being identical to him or herself over time) and *relational identification* (which sees identity as resulting from a process whereby a person is said to be the same as, or other to, socio-culturally available narratives). On the basis of these distinctions we next turn to identity politics and explore how narrative approaches to identity can be used to understand the cultural and political contestations over identity. Finally, we review our discussion in terms of its implications for how teacher and student identities may or may not be produced in connection with pedagogical practices.

Reflexive and relational narrative identification

We wish to begin by considering how narrative identities are formed. To do so we draw on a number of authors who have developed narrative perspectives and theorisations of identity (in particular Gergen and Gergen 1988; Somers and Gibson 1994) and bring them together to (re)tell a story about narrative identification. In doing this, we distinguish between two interdependent processes of identification – one that we call reflexive identification and the other that we call relational identification. By reflexive identification we refer to the way that people can reflexively construct their own identities through processes of self-narration. This is the process by which a given person can create for themselves a life history or 'self narrative' (Gergen and Gergen 1988). By relational identification we refer to the way that, in constructing a self-narrative, people draw on narrative resources that are available outside of their self. Thus, although a self-narrative can be developed to appear that it is the unique property of a person (e.g. *I* am a unique, self-contained individual), in practice that identity draws on social and cultural definitions of possible identities (i.e. the identity position *I* associate with *my*self pre-exists *me*). Hence any individual identity always *relates* to forms of identity that predate it being narrated.

To begin, we first make some general comments on the characteristics associated with narrative *per se*, and subsequently we describe in more detail the nature and relationships between processes of reflexive and relational identification.

Generally speaking, a narrative comprises an ordered series of events that plot the 'transformation from an initial situation to a terminal situation' (Ricoeur 1992: 141). What this points to is that two important features of narrative are time and change – a narrative is by definition a temporalisation of events that involve change. Further,

such a temporalisation is structured through a process of emplotment
– the joining together of disparate events into a structure. Emplotment
thus gives significance to independent instances that include the demonstration of a chain of causality between those events; hence, the
plot is the logic of the narrative (Somers and Gibson 1994). Therefore, in the narrative 'we teach and they learn' there is a process of
causal emplotment that suggests that the pedagogic activities of the
teacher are causally related to the learning outcomes of the students.
Through this process of emplotment emerges another characteristic
of narrative – the theme. Thus, plots are thematised such that events
are selectively appropriated in order that they can be normatively
evaluated (Somers and Gibson 1994).

In addition to the thematisation and causality constructed through
narrative, narrative also relies on characterisation. Here narrative
relates a character to a plot such that 'telling a story is saying who
did what and how, by spreading out in time the connection between
these various viewpoints' (Ricoeur 1992: 146). Hence, in narrative
terms, identity is the identity of the characters of the story that are
constructed in connection with the construction of the plot of a story.
Narrative thus emplots and thematises events in the world through
the dynamic concept of identity. It is here that the idea of narrative
identity emerges from the way that people are constituted in narratives as particular types of people. Identity can thus be formed by
assessing one's relation with characters in narratives – either by identifying with them or by seeing them as different to oneself. Thus one
can construct an identity both through a process of 'sameness' and
a process of 'otherness'. The further implication is that identity is
active – it is a form of identification – such that people can identify or
not identify with particular narrative characters in defining who they
are in relation to others.

In reflecting on such processes of narration and identification, how
can identity be said to be constructed narratively? First, it is worth
noting that the very notion of identity implies a sense of sameness
– for two things to be identical means that there is no difference
between them. In terms of personal identity, then, in what sense is
identity 'the same as' something else? One perspective suggests that
the answer is that an identity is somehow stable over time such that
who one is today is recognisable the same as who one was last week,
last month, last year and so forth. Here identity has a temporal unity
across the span of a life but it should not be seen as reducible to
'identical' (see McLeod 2000 which discusses two individuals and

their constructions of self over the eight years of the study). Another reading of identity suggests that people can be said to have an identity in so far as they are identified with particular ways of being. For example, a person might identify with his or her profession and therefore that profession becomes part of his or her identity. Such identifications involve practices as well as thoughts – for example, a person who identifies as being a 'student' does at least some of a range of activities involved with being a student: reads, studies, attends classes, enrols and sits exams etc. We refer to these two readings as 'reflexive identity' and 'relational identity'.

Reflexive identity is achieved when a person sees himself or herself as having a temporal unity, and relational identity is achieved when a person defines himself or herself in terms of a socially or discursively recognised identity. For narrative identity these two processes work together in the process of identity formation such that a reflexive identity, rather than being an essence, or innate and unchanging is only achieved though a process of relational identification with socially available narratives. A person's identity is thus both centred and decentred, such that although one can say 'I am me', the 'me' that is referred to is always constructed out of socially and culturally available narrative identities and their attendant practices.

What we have termed here reflexive identification is the process through which people come to see themselves as unique individuals who have an identity that 'belongs' to them. This process allows a person to identify with themselves – so, for example, in western culture it is common for us to talk of a 'life story' which emplots the events of one's life in such a way as to construct the person as a unique individual whose identity, at least in part, endures through that story. Hence, people can talk about their lives, and they can write biographies and autobiographies that provide a narrative continuity to one life that constructs a person as having an identity that endures through time. Here, identity is developed through 'self-narratives' (Gergen and Gergen 1988; McLeod 2000, 2001) that purport to be representational and to recount a person's life history and their part in it as an 'identity'. This suggests that people have the ability to be reflexive – to look at themselves as if being outside of themselves. To do so positions a person as a temporal being who has a future (where one is ahead of oneself), a past (where one has been) and a present (where one is with oneself) (Binswanger 1958). The implication of such a temporalisation is that identity is narrated – it positions a person as having an existence that endures through time and that can be positioned temporally. Further, this means that the notion of identity exists in the nexus between difference (temporal) and sameness (identical) – *I was, I am, I will be* (McLeod 2000 is a good illustration of this).

This process of reflexive identification is one that purports that identity is contained within a 'representational narrative' (Somers and Gibson 1994) – one that claims to represent the events of the past and will continue into the future. Following Somers and Gibson, in this sense, a story relates to a description and repetition of past events. Such a notion of representation implies that to represent 'carries the dual connotation of making present to the mind and the senses whilst standing for something that is not present'. Acts of representation thus enable us to deal with 'absence as an imagined presence' (Simpson 1997: 54). In contemporary theory there has been much debate about the ability of 'representations' to unproblematically represent and duplicate reality, to the extent that it has been suggested that there is a 'profound uncertainty about what constitutes an adequate description of social "reality"' (Lather 1991: 21). Notwithstanding such uncertainty, representational narratives, even when they denounce such duplication, still define themselves in terms of their relative (in)ability to reflect the real (Rhodes 2001). Hence, reflexive identification might be an ongoing struggle through which a person relates to, and finds a place in, the world that they experience.

In suggesting such an 'endurance' of identity through self-narration, it is not our position that identity is essential, but rather that people can use narrative to create an image of endurance such that narrative is a resource for the self. Of course, the self-narrative one tells today can be expected to be different to the one told in the future and each may construct differently an enduring notion of identity. Thus, in agreement with Hall (1996), we suggest that having an identity does not mean having an unchanging core self that is identical to itself through time. Rather, our point is that self-narratives are important in that they can be used to posit such an identity (however ephemeral), and that this process is important to how identities are formed.

To accept that people can reflexively construct their identities through autobiographical acts which assume a sense of identity constancy over time does not imply that those identities are the sole property of the person who narrates them. The process of relational identification is such that the resources which are used to define a 'self' reflexively are not of that self's own making – they are borrowed from socially available 'ontological narratives' (Somers and Gibson 1994; see also McLeod 2000, 2001). These ontological narratives can be defined as the 'stories that social actors use to make sense of . . . their lives' (Somers and Gibson 1994: 62) such that how a person identifies themselves within such narratives endows them with an identity. Such ontological narratives are social and interpersonal such that people's identities are constructed through the narrative to the extent that they locate themselves within, or against, available emplotted stories. Thus, 'it is through narrativity that we come to know, understand, and make sense of the social world, and it is through narratives and narrativity that we constitute out identities' (Somers and Gibson 1994: 59). An ontological narrative, a narrative of *being*, does not necessarily claim to represent actual or historical events, nor does it claim to present a singular rational process. Rather, we use it here to refer to an exemplary story which contains characters that people may identify with. Hence a narrative notion of identity suggests that a person's identity is created through its location and identification within social narratives that are not of that person's making.

Although the distinction between reflexive and relational narration that we make is analytically useful in theorising narrative identity, it is important to realise that a process of narrative identity formation cannot neatly separate the two processes. We have tried to disentangle these processes in order to develop a useful understanding of them – however, they are in practice still inextricably entangled. Although a person might relationally identify with ontological narratives as a resource through which they define themselves, such identification can also be used by that person as a means of representing himself or herself in a 'self-narrative'. In this sense a 'self-narrative' is an 'individual's account of the relationship among self-relevant events across time . . . [through which] . . . the individual attempts to establish coherent connections amongst life events' (Gergen and Gergen 1988: 19). Such narratives are symbolic systems through which people are able to negotiate their lives and through which they can justify or criticise themselves and others. For a person to claim or be associated with a particular identity, the narrative resources that enable such a definition must already be available and be in cultural circulation.

It is also important to note that the perspective we are putting forward sees identity as dynamic and always in process – it is defined through a process of identification where one's self-narratives can be retold through the incorporation of different ontologies and where those ontologies can themselves change through their usage. So, for example, a person can identify themselves as a teacher or as a student and tell a story that positions them as such a person, but to do so implies that these categories of person are already available for them to identify with. Further, this availability is made possible through the various ontological narratives of student and teacher identity that exist – narratives that provide models of different types of behaviour and that themselves change over time. By implication, selfhood is seen not as a property of 'mind' but rather is located on the boundaries between selfhood and otherness – it is liminal and becoming, and always includes the voices of others (de Peuter 1998). Self-narratives can thus only ever be multi-voiced as a person comes to define him or herself through the ontological narratives she or he learns from others. Identity is formed in the dynamic interplay between reflexive and relational processes of identification. For example, a person might think of themselves as a teacher and thus claim this category as part of his or her identity because she or he participates in the attendant practices, histories and relations associated with the category of teacher. Such a person, however, did not invent the notion of 'teacher' – the category must exist prior to anyone being able to use it to identify themselves, even if the associations of the category change over time. Thus it is through the (changing) practice of teaching that one can claim to be teacher. As such, the various ontological narratives in which teachers are depicted provide people with resources with which to define themselves as such. Lyotard (1984: 15) sums this up nicely:

> No self is an island; each exists in a fabric of relations . . . even before he is born, if only by virtue of the name he is given, the human child is already positioned as the referent in the story recounted by those around him, in relation to which he will inevitably chart his course.

It is to the socio-political dimension of how such a course may be charted that we now turn.

Identity politics

So far, we have argued for a conceptualisation of identity that combines the interplay between reflexive and relational processes of identification. Now we turn the discussion to the implications of this view for the political dimensions of identity. As Rose (1996) argues, in one sense the idea that identity is narrative can be used to assume that narratives are merely a resource which people can use; hence narratives might be thought of as providing discursively established vocabularies that play a part in who people come to see themselves as. This can assume that people can unproblematically 'choose' from the variety of available narratives in order to define themselves. Further, Rose's point is that such a 'choice' based argument still requires that there is a humanistic 'I' who remains as the one who makes these selections as if from a menu of possibilities.

Concurring with Rose, our perspective acknowledges that identity, while not pre-given or totally determined, is not something that is 'free floating'. For one thing, as we have argued, when taking a narrative approach to identity formation, an identity is social in that it is constructed through the ontological narratives that are available – a person's relative uniqueness may contingently emerge through the different narratives they use to define themselves and the way that those narratives are used, but the narratives can never wholly originate from and be unique to that person. The narratives one uses to form an identity are used in way that is mediated through power – dominant narratives are such because they enjoin with practices of inclusion and exclusion that enable them to retain their dominance. Also, particular identities are only available in relation to others – so, for example, the location of a person within the identity of either man or woman has a significant influence on which other identities may be available. For example, men and women can now take up a wider range of professional identities than in the past. This draws attention to the historically changing narrative resources available for identity formation.

Nevertheless, to the extent that there is choice in defining oneself, this choice is not unencumbered. Some ontological narratives impose themselves on one's identity with different degrees of voracity than others. For example, there are various forms of public narrative attached to cultural and institutional formations – families, workplaces, churches, governments etc. – within which people are socially compelled to define themselves (Somers and Gibson 1994). Further, what Lyotard (1984) terms 'grand narratives' – such as progress, emancipation, enlightenment etc. – also exact a power against which people must contend in order for their identities to be formed. Such grand narratives have as their goal the legitimation of social and political institutions and practices, laws, ethics and ways of thinking and acting by making a claim to universality (Lyotard 1992).

Rose (1996) makes the point that the importance of using a broadly discursive (in our case narrative) means of understanding identity relates not to what such narratives *mean*, but rather to what they *do* – i.e. what forms of identity they do and do not permit or promote. Invoking a narrative perspective of the self can thus be used to suggest that narratives, and the identities they conjure, can only exist with what Foucault (1980) calls 'regimes of truth'. Here such regimes are socially constituted discourses that embody a politics of truth – discourses that define what can function as being true and what can be thought possible or sayable. Such regimes similarly help to define identity in terms of which 'types' of people are said to be able to function as acceptable identities and which might be considered undesirable, deviant, punishable or worthy of social excommunication. Hence 'which kinds of narrative will socially predominate is contested politically and will depend in large part on the distribution of power' (Somers and Gibson 1994: 73). Further, the interconnections and imposed limitations of political elements of different narratives are what constitute identity politics.

Identity politics, in its various expressions, is 'constituted by people who previously felt marginalised from dominant political channels and more mainstream political movements' (Somers and Gibson 1994). Identity politics is a label used when groups *claim* identifications around 'difference' of some sort: race, ethnicity, gender, disability, sexuality. A key part of such movements is to reject the narratives of identity that had been ascribed to them (as inferior, or lesser), and to claim and construct new narratives which did not work primarily in terms of an inferior other. A second issue is the taking on of identity as a prime site of political struggle: to see the taken-for-granted dominant narrative identity of the putative social actor (white, male, western, straight etc.) as an important form of power and source of subordination.

Concluding remarks: narrative, identity and pedagogy

In terms of the identity positions available within pedagogical discourse our discussion of narrative and identity politics highlights, and intends to open to question, a particular aspect of traditional perspectives on pedagogy.

Pedagogy is political in the way it provides an identity resource which people might adopt or resist in their own self-narration. This can be productive in that it might offer people new positions through which to define themselves, but it can also be repressive when it works to limit or censure alternatives to those positions. This is indeed an important and troublesome aspect of pedagogy – one that attempts to co-opt people's identities by setting up very particular alternatives as those that people should strive towards: the powerful desire either for others to be like ourselves or for others to become like those exemplars we set out for them. Indeed, even the most 'open', humanistic, liberated and/or experiential pedagogies presuppose a particular type of desirable subject/identity. This echoes the tradition that pedagogy assumes that people's minds, as they are given, both should be (and have to be) reformed by the educator (Lyotard 1992). In this sense education has always been about 'disciplining and binding in to the social order' (Wexler 1995: 75). The political question is one that relates to how the identities to which people are 'reformed' are defined and which other identities are either privileged or marginalised in the process.

This political dimension of pedagogical narrative identity is thus about who people are (or are not) able to be and whether particular people are (or are not) included in particular narratives of identity. For those engaged in pedagogy, this implies a responsibility to question how different practices legitimise particular identities and what are the effects of such legitimations – these are some of the issues that are dealt with in subsequent chapters. Hence, looking to identity as narrative, and relating this to pedagogy, enables a discussion of pedagogy that draws attention to its cultural political dimensions (including our own complicity in this power). This is not to suggest that the pedagogical power to change identity is necessarily negative or repressive, but rather to invoke the potential for reflexivity to be brought into the processes through which pedagogy changes identity.

We have argued in this chapter that identity is a result of both reflexive and relational processes of identification. A narrative perspective on identity as we have described it implies that no identity is possible without relational reference to ontological narratives. In this sense it is inconceivable that a person can exist as a self in a way that bears no reference or relation to something outside of that self – to have an identity is to be able to define oneself in terms of the 'other'; identity is social, not personal. One cannot envisage a person who has a unique identity that in no way resembles the identity of anyone else. Indeed, identity is important because it links people to the societies in which they live such that 'representation as a cultural practice establishes individual and collective identities and symbolic systems provide possible answers to the questions: who am I? what could

I be? who do I want to be?' (Woodward 1997: 14). Pedagogy is a means whereby people might learn new ways of identifying relationally in order develop new forms of reflexive identity.

Thus, narrative identity can be seen to be positioned in an indeterminate space between exteriority and interiority. It is an identity that both claims to be unique and individuated yet must exist through the narratives of others. One can thus see the practice of pedagogy, in these terms, as that which invokes change within the restrictions of this indeterminacy. If pedagogy did not involve any change to the people involved, then there would be no learning and it would be no pedagogy at all. Different pedagogies will, to differing degrees, seek to colonise people within particular identities while enabling (or restricting) distinct identities to emerge. Pedagogy is thus inevitably political. Whereas identities construct places from which people can position themselves and from which they can speak (Woodward 1997) the question turns to the ways in which pedagogy does (and does not) construct opportunities for different ways of speaking and being.

In many ways, the subsequent chapters of this book explore such politics by examining specific pedagogic practices related to organisational culture, gender, sexuality, higher education, organisations, popular culture etc. An important question that a narrative theorisation of identity poses for pedagogy relates to how particular pedagogical practices create or suppress different narratives which in turn have political implications for who people can or cannot be.

Chapter 4

Pedagogies for personal change in the 'self-help' literature

Helping oneself

Introduction

In this chapter we explore the nature of the pedagogy embedded in much of the 'self-help' literature. Arguably the idea of self-help for personal change can be seen as part of a growing self-help ethos in other aspects of contemporary life. First, there is the familiar range of 'self-service' consumer provisions, from the early self-service features of supermarkets and petrol stations to the technology-based self-services in banking, travel, entertainment and even taxation self-assessment. Second, in the contemporary workplace, there is a demand for flexible, innovative, multi-skilled and entrepreneurial workers who have a capacity to monitor their performance, be reflexive, self-regulate and align their 'selves' with the strategic goals of the organisation. Included here are the increasing numbers of 'portfolio' workers (Gee 2000; see also Chapter 5) who do not have organisational allegiances but who are conscious of building their 'portfolio' of skills to maintain their position in the labour market. Third, in contemporary education, there has been a marked shift from 'teaching' to 'learning', with a corresponding demand placed on learners to be more active in their learning. This translates into learners being more 'self-directed' and 'self-reflective', and it includes self-assessment and the ongoing monitoring of progress. The advent of 'e-learning' is another manifestation of the self-service features of contemporary education. Finally, there is a great deal of sociological commentary on the changing nature of the self and its relations with broader society. For example, Rose (1996: 164) observes that, in the last 25 years or so, there has been a shift in the relationship between the citizen and his or her community. In the first half of the twentieth century, he argues, '[t]he individual was a locus of needs that were to be socially met if malign consequences were to be avoided, but was

reciprocally to be a being to whom political, civil, and social obligations and duties were to be attached' – pedagogical technologies from
universal education to the BBC were devices for forming responsible
citizens. In contrast, 'There is now an emphasis on personal choice,
individual freedom, self fulfilment and initiative – citizenship is active
and individualistic rather than passive and dependent' (p. 165) and

> The self steering capacities of individuals are now construed as
> vital resources for achieving private profit, public tranquillity and
> social progress, and interventions in these areas have also come
> to be guided by the regulatory norm of the autonomous, respons-
> ible subject, obliged to make its life meaningful through act of
> choice.
>
> (p. 160)

Our broad interest then (in this chapter and the book), is in life as
an enterprise of the self (Gordon 1991), and the techniques deployed
to foster self-awareness, self-presentation, self-esteem and self-change.
In particular, how do pedagogies proceed to constitute a positive new
self? And how are traditional techniques in religion and philosophy,
such as self-reflection, self-examination, renunciation, confession,
abstinence and so on, modified for the new purpose of the enter-
prising self?

Our particular approach in this chapter is to explore the practices
of 'self-work' apparent in the self-help genre, their purpose, and the
way in which such practices inscribe learners as certain 'sorts' of
persons. Such practices can be seen as 'technologies of the self'
(Foucault 1988) as described in Chapter 1. Our concern is with practices in which persons are understood and acted upon rather than
with the theoretical ideas about persons, which are promulgated in
the self-help literature. Following Rose (1996: 23) we are interested
in investigating practices and techniques 'of thought as it seeks to
make itself technical'.

As a way into this task, a selection of self-help books are analysed
in terms of how readers are invited to 'act upon themselves'. The
general position adopted is that, despite the variety of practices
evident in the self-help literature, such practices have in common the
goal of producing psychological subjects characterised by an autonomous, stable, coherent and unified 'self'.

The enterprise of self-help books

It is important to understand self-help books as commercial enterprises in their own right. In a recent anthology of 50 self-help books, Butler-Bowden (2001) estimates they have combined sales exceeding 150 million copies. One of the 'best sellers' in this genre, Stephen Covey's *The 7 Habits of Highly Effective People* (1990), has sold over a million copies a year for the last 13 years, and has been translated into 32 languages.

Typically, a host of enterprises are built around the more successful self-help books. Thus we read on the back cover of his book that Stephen Covey is 'co-chairman of Franklin Covey Co, which is involved in leadership development worldwide with over 300 of the Fortune 500 companies' and that Anthony Robbins (*Awaken the Giant Within*, 1992) is an 'extraordinarily successful entrepreneur and the founder of nine companies. He has been a consultant to business governments in the United States and abroad'. Self-help books are typically only one aspect of a larger merchandising strategy which includes videos, public workshops, corporate change programmes (see Chapter 6), television and radio appearances and of course companion or 'sequel' volumes. Thus the authors of self-help books present themselves as exemplars of their message: by following their prescribed precepts and practices, they are demonstrably both financially and personally successful (no matter that in most instances their financial success is principally based on royalties from sales of self-help books!).

Although self-help books typically draw on a wide range of ideas – from religion, philosophy, history, psychology and autobiography – three areas predominate and serve to shape their thinking: organisational psychology (including leadership); psychological, therapeutic and counselling practices; and what have been termed 'new age' ideas, which typically blend eastern and western religion and philosophy. It is also worth noting that self-help authors, perhaps unwittingly, are also exemplars of their gender: compare titles by male authors such as *The 7 Habits of Highly Effective People*, *Awaken the Giant Within* and *How to Win Friends and Influence People* (Carnegie 1999) (with their external, instrumental and even manipulative focus, and/or obviously phallic connotations) with titles by female authors such as *Life Makeovers* (Richardson 2001), *You Can Heal Your Life* (Hay 1987) and *Self-esteem Workbook: An Interactive Approach to Changing Your Life* (Field 2001) (with their more personal and internal focus).

Despite the diversity of influences on self-help books there is remarkable uniformity in their message to readers: that it is possible to blend personal prosperity and personal fulfilment, and to create and manage a 'persona' while at the same time maintaining authenticity as a human being. It is ironic then that self-help books often present themselves as anti-money and success oriented, and even as anti-conformity. Indeed, there is a discernible 'move' in the early parts of many self-help books to define the 'problem', and this typically takes the form of anecdotes (or parables) which illustrate how people can be distracted from their true authentic selves by being caught up in the pursuit of material wealth and professional advancement.

For example, in the opening chapter of *The 7 Habits*, Covey (1990: 15) relates the following:

> I've set and met my career goals and I'm having tremendous professional success. But it's cost me my personal and family life. I don't know my wife and children any more. I'm not even sure I know myself and what's really important to me. I've had to ask myself – is it worth it?

Similarly, in the Introduction to *Life Makeovers* Richardson (2001: 2) describes a number of situations where a 'life makeover' may be prescribed:

> in David's situation, his success has given him much more than he bargained for. Sitting at his desk at the end of a busy day David wonders if all his hard work is really paying off. His consulting business is more successful than ever. He's made more money this year than in the last two years combined . . . yet David walks around with a nagging feeling that something is missing . . . Instead of feeling happy about the role he's created for himself, David says he feels like an employee working for everyone else . . . David's not sure he is willing to continue paying such a high price for success.

So, self-help books seem to be at least partially targeted towards those who have had conventionally successful lives, who have worked hard, conformed to the expectations placed upon them and have had career or business success with accompanying material well-being, but who are nevertheless searching for more balance in their lives. Thus they typically build on stories that are familiar to readers, stories with which they identify and regard as true of them. The prescriptions in the self-help literature are anti-conformity only in the sense that they stress the need to avoid living one's life according to the expectations of others; and they are anti-material only in the sense that a focus on external material gains needs to be replaced with a focus on the unique qualities of the self. They reverse the equation so that material gain and the approval of others are a natural outcome of living an authentic and self-aware life. This is well illustrated in *The Seven Spiritual Laws of Success* by Deepak Chopra (1996: 109) who is quite explicit in his approach to wealth:

> The Seven Spiritual Laws of Success are powerful principles that will enable you to attain self-mastery. If you put your attention on these laws and practice the steps outlined in this book, you will see that you can manifest anything that you want – all the affluence, money and success that you desire. You will also see that your life becomes more joyful and abundant in every way, for these laws are also the spiritual laws of life that make living worthwhile.

Earlier, Chopra outlines the need to focus internally, to discover one's true self:

> The experience of the Self, or 'self-referral', means that our internal reference point is our own spirit, and not the objects of our experience. The opposite of self-referral is object-referral. In object referral we are constantly seeking the approval of others . . . In object referral, your internal reference point is your ego. The ego, however, is not who you really are. The ego is your self-image, it is your social mask; it is the role you are playing. Your social mask thrives on approval. It wants to control, and it is sustained by power, because it lives in fear . . . Your true self, which is your spirit, your soul, is completely free of those things.
>
> (1996: 11)

This is typical of the self-help literature: it draws on the binaries of inner-outer, material-spiritual, and past-future. Whatever the problem, the solution is the same: to focus internally and discover, unearth or otherwise construct a more independent, autonomous, freely-choosing self. And so the first step to self-renewal and transformation is self-awareness, and it is here that different pedagogical devices are located.

Exemplars of the self-help literature

Covey has a universal view of human development: that it is a process of moving from dependence to independence, and finally to interdependence. In fact this view of development is what drives the construction of *The 7 Habits*. The first three habits deal with self-mastery – i.e. moving from dependence to independence (also referred to as a 'private victory'), while habits 4–6 deal with the development of interdependence (also referred to as a 'public victory'). Covey's pedagogy is clearly directed towards the construction of a self-aware, independent (and interdependent), autonomous and freely-choosing individual. His habits are principally injunctions to be followed: 'be proactive', 'begin with the end in mind', 'put first things first', 'think win-win', 'seek first to understand, then to be understood', 'synergise' and 'sharpen the saw'. Significantly it is through the practice of these habits that self awareness and mastery is achieved, and so Covey spends a great deal of his book on motivating the reader to practise the relevant habit, and providing them with everyday exercises or tips to 'self-diagnose' existing habits and then to 'correct' those habits. For example, with habit 1 he invokes us to 'listen to our language' and provides examples of 'reactive' and 'proactive' language:

Reactive language	Proactive language
There's nothing I can do	Let's look at our alternatives
That's just the way I am	I can choose a different approach
They won't allow that	I can create an effective presentation
I have to do that	I will choose an appropriate response

Accompanying this self-diagnosis is a set of exercises or 'drills' to maintain and strengthen the habit. The same approach is used for all seven habits. Covey's approach to personal change has the following elements:

1   A singular view of the end point of self-change – the autonomous, choosing individual.
2   A motive for change, normally encapsulated by the idea that life is not entirely fulfilling because of the perceived need to live according to the expectations and scripts of others.
3   A regime of change built around the everyday practice of habits, which are ultimately 'character forming'.

A similar approach can be found in Anthony Robbins' *Awaken the Giant Within*. He advocates the use of what he terms 'neuro-associative conditioning', which is a formula-driven process for changing behavioural habits. The six steps of neuro-associative conditioning are:

1   Decide what you really want and what's preventing you from having it now.
2   Get leverage: associate massive pain to not changing it now and massive pleasure to the experience of changing now!
3   Interrupt the limiting pattern.
4   Create a new empowering alternative.
5   Condition the new pattern until it's consistent.
6   Test it!

An excerpt from step 5 illustrates the flavour of his approach:

> If you rehearse the new, empowering alternative again and again with tremendous emotional intensity, you'll carve out a pathway, and with even more repetition and emotion, it will become a part of your habitual behavior. Remember, your brain can't tell the difference between something you vividly imagine and something you actually experience.
>
> (Robbins 1992: 137)

Like Covey, Robbins recognises the power of words in personal transformation and many of his exercises are built around substituting new words for old in one's vocabulary. For example, in the chapter 'The Vocabulary of Ultimate Success' he reminds us to '[r]emember that your brain loves anything that gets you out of pain and into pleasure, so pick a word that you'll want to use in place of the old, limiting one' (p. 216). He then produces a long list of possible positive replacement words and their negative counterparts, a sample of which are:

Negative emotion/expression: I'm feeling . . .	Transforms into: I'm feeling . . .
Anxious	Expectant
Dread	Challenge
Failure	Learning
Lazy	Storing energy
Lost	Searching
Fearful	Curious
Stressed	Energised

Robbins also has exercises that promote the ongoing monitoring of progress. One such exercise he calls 'Yesterday, today and to-morrow', the idea being to allocate a score and a short description to each of ten critical areas of life five years ago. His instructions for this exercise are:

> next to each of these categories, give yourself a score on a scale from 0 to 10, 0 meaning you had nothing in this area, and 10 meaning you were absolutely living your life's desire in that category . . . write a sentence next to each category to describe what you were like back then.
>
> (1992: 276)

The ten categories are: 'physically', 'mentally', 'emotionally', 'relation-ships', 'attractiveness', 'living environment', 'socially', 'spiritually', 'career' and 'financially'. Robbins then invites the reader to repeat the exercise for today and five years hence, and to reflect on what has been learned from the comparison of the three.

In another exercise, Robbins implores readers to identify their per-sonal, career, material and 'contribution' goals. He provides some questions to prompt readers' visualisation of a better future – for example, under 'goals' he asks variously:

> What would you want to learn? Study the violin with virtuoso Itzak Pearlman? What do you want to earn? $10 million a year? What would you like to purchase? A private zoo stocked with

giraffes, alligators, and hippos? How could you contribute? [i.e. to the lives of others and society] Read to the blind? Halt the destruction of the rainforests? Eliminate racial discrimination?

(1992: 300)

Following these questions Robbins advises:

so perhaps the key question is 'What kind of person will I have to become in order to achieve all that I want? . . . take a moment now and write a paragraph describing all the character traits, skills, abilities, attitudes, and beliefs that you would need to develop in order to achieve all of the goals you've written down previously.

(1992: 303)

It is interesting to compare the question posed by Robbins with Foucault's paraphase of Weber: 'If one wants to behave rationally and regulate one's actions according to true principles, what part of oneself should one renounce?' (1988: 17) and with Foucault himself 'what must one know about oneself in order to be willing to renounce anything?' (1988: 17). For Robbins the focus is on creating a new self. In this context, renunciation is not a matter of sacrificing aspects of one's true nature, it is only a matter of renunciating patterns of behaviour which have hitherto constrained one's self – there is no sense of the ascetic here. But there is a sense in which knowledge of the self precedes any future construction of the self: i.e. a knowledge of 'limiting patterns' of behaviour and an unanalysed knowledge of one's wants.

Robbins' approach to change involves a combination of substituting new behaviours for old, visualisation of a better future, and personal strategic planning. His version of knowing oneself is knowing the limiting patterns and thought processes that have hitherto shackled any personal fulfilment. Such knowledge is followed by renunciation of such patterns and the pursuit of a regime of behaviour and language focusing on goals that have no limits. Writing is an important device for 'knowing oneself' but it does not lead to any realistic self-appraisal; its function is to identify and renounce past patterns of living and to identify and embrace goals for the future, without any limits. The explicit position is that we are in control of our self-change and transformation and whatever goals we set are attainable.

Both Covey and Robbins begin their seminal works with an explicit philosophy of life. Covey, for example, refers to the need to develop a 'character ethic' and to live life according to 'self-evident' principles such as fairness, integrity, honesty, human dignity, service, quality, and so on: 'principles are deep fundamental truths that have universal application . . . they're fundamental. They're essentially un-arguable because they are self evident' (1998: 35). Similarly, Robbins (1992: 23), in pursuing the 'dream', offers us:

> three elementary principles of change that you and I can use immediately to change our lives. While these principles are sim-ple, they are also extremely powerful when they are skillfully applied. These are the exact same changes that an individual must make in order to create personal change, that a company must make in order to maximise is potential, and that a country must make in order to carve out its place in the world.

Even though both are concerned with opening up possibilities in people's lives and are hostile to 'quick fix' superficial solutions, ultim-ately they resort to rather simple 'fundamental truths' as being the engine of personal change. And in the case of Robbins at least, these truths apply to the triptych of personal, organisational and social change.

In contrast to the rather grand approach of Covey and Robbins, Lynda Field's *Self-esteem Workbook* (2001) has no explicit philo-sophy to which readers must subscribe. Instead she moves very quickly into the business of personal change through a series of self-assessment exercises. Part 1 of her book is titled 'A Personal Assess-ment of Your Present Levels of Self-esteem'. The exercises focus on three areas: thinking, feeling and behaving. They draw upon readers' experiences in a number of ways. For example, one exercise requires readers to 'Think of a time when you felt high in self-esteem and then something occurred which totally demoralized you' (p. 11). Ques-tions then follow which construct the experience in terms of feelings, thoughts and behaviour. The possibility of alternatives is explored, followed by a self-esteem checklist and then a visualisation exercise relating to an instance of high self-esteem. The checklist is one of many throughout the book, the final one typifying the approach, having a number of areas which the reader is asked to rank from 1 to 7, 1 being 'totally depressed, utterly miserable' and 7 being 'delighted, thrilled, very happy'. The areas relate to aspects of life such as friends, partners, family, creativity, health, fitness, success, recognition and so on.

This constant measuring of self-esteem is in contrast to the visualisation exercise, the instructions for which are as follows:

> Find a quiet space and sit comfortably. Take some deep breaths and relax your body. Now; remember a time when you were high in self-esteem – it doesn't matter how long ago this time was. Close your eyes and see yourself in this confident, relaxed mode. Try to remember the details of this experience. Where were you? Who was with you? What did you feel like? Imagine that you are recreating those exact feelings . . .
>
> (Field 2001: 21)

An exercise such as this is similar to techniques in narrative therapy, where clients are encouraged to think of 'counter instances' to a current problem. In this instance, if the 'problem' is self-esteem, then focusing on counter instances helps to built hope, possibility and the prospect of rewriting the narratives about oneself. As Field exhorts: 'we are what we believe we are'. Throughout Field's book the reader is constantly asked to identify experiences and to think about them in terms of how they felt, thought and behaved. Thus there is an interesting combination of 'measurement' for the purpose of diagnosis, reflections/analysis of past experiences, visualisation of positive experiences and the creation of new positive images for oneself.

Pedagogical practices

We have presented the above examples as illustrations of different pedagogical practices, but they clearly lie at the intersection of pedagogy/counselling/therapy, and this is to be expected where learning is so obviously connected with significant personal change. A common element in all the texts is the idea of reflection on experience, but for different purposes and using different strategies. We now return to the question of how readers of the self-help literature are invited to 'act upon themselves'. In response to this, a variety of practices can be discerned around the following ways of relating to oneself.

Knowing oneself

One version of this is the calculable subject, the deployment of measuring practices to ascertain 'normality' and to identify deficits, such as deficits in self-esteem, or deficits in feelings of success, or the lack of a 'dream'. Another version is the range of introspective 'self-reflective' practices, often carried out in groups and involving, say, the sharing of ideas and stories or the surfacing of beliefs and assumptions (which may involve locating the social, cultural and psychological constraints that govern our behaviour with the aim of rescuing subjectivity from social repression). Typical of these is the 'I should' exercise used by both Louise Hay and Lynda Field, whereby the 'shoulds' of life (representing the psychological constraints in one's life) are listed and challenged. Another interpretation of 'knowing oneself' is to know the 'human condition', which is certainly a practice exploited by Covey.

Controlling oneself

This revolves around the notion of mastery and the exercise of authority over oneself (i.e. self-regulation). 'Tools' include time management, documenting actions, setting work goals, the daily planner, the personal organiser, measuring outcomes, personal performance management, the rewriting and construction of one's life goals and the containment or alignment of one's expressed beliefs and values with the 'mission' or 'vision' of an organisation. Discipline is a key feature of many self-help texts, with the emphasis on the need to 'practise' a daily regime of habits or exercises so that personal change is cemented into daily routines.

Caring for oneself (paying attention to oneself, watching oneself)

Confessional practices, cathartic experiences, stress management, regimes around physical fitness, diet, personal health and hygiene, exploration of relationships at home and in the workplace, empowerment and learning how to manage the demands of work are all techniques and approaches aimed at happiness, well-being and self development. Practices evident in the self-help literature are those such as writing letters to oneself, diary writing, the exploration of self-image and values, the documentation of critical life events or incidents, journaling, life history exploration, exploration of own needs (emotional, intellectual, social and spiritual) and identification of the conditions which facilitate growth (the creative person and the motivated person who has been lost – 'cleansing the doors of perception' etc.).

(Re)creating oneself

Practices here include confession (critical self-disclosure) followed by renunciation and then the affirmation of a new identity. Other practices involve challenging and changing beliefs and assumptions (which may involve some kind of ideology critique), and development of 'replacement narratives'. Many self-help texts, including the examples given above, recognise the power of language and the need to recreate oneself through 're-languaging' – whether this involves relabelling or rewriting.

Concluding comments

In its various forms the self-help literature uniformly promotes self-management towards an active, autonomous, choosing self. Arguably the pedagogical practices deployed can be seen as self-regulatory devices upon which the contemporary notion of an 'enterprise culture' draws. For example, one facet of an enterprise culture is the need for organisational change and renewal. Such change invariably demands a re-examination and reorientation of workers' organisational knowledge (tacit, explicit and cultural). Such a demand can be conceptualised as a 'calling forth' of new worker identities. Leaders, for example, are exhorted to move from 'command and control' styles towards a more collaborative style. Workers are exhorted to be more flexible, multiskilled and self-reflective, with 'flexibility' including a willingness and capacity to take on new identities as they are demanded (e.g. when there is a corporate takeover or merger, or a move from bureaucratic to more entrepreneurial activities, or where there are new technologies and work practices being introduced, and so on). Thus in the name of 'learning for change' workers are invited, encouraged or otherwise cajoled into a great deal of 'self-work' (self-examination, self-reflection, self-regulation). However, the reflective practices so pervasive in the literature are certainly not reflexive practices as understood by Edwards *et al.* (2002) (see p. 3 of the Introduction). And they lie outside the reflexivity typically associated with the practices of 'conscientisation' (Freire 1972) 'consciousness raising' (Hart 1990) and 'perspective transformation' (Mezirow 1991). In this context, the self-help literature can be seen as offering the illusion of autonomy and choice within a regime of self-governance.

Chapter 5

Writing portfolios in a work-based learning programme

Textually producing oneself

Introduction

The purpose of this chapter is to explore one of the new pedagogies of self that has an increasing currency in universities today. This new pedagogy involves the writing of individual learning portfolios. The portfolios that are of interest here are located within a set of work-based learning (WBL) programmes at a university in Australia. In this university, WBL programmes refer to a set of postgraduate degrees where learners' work, work experience and workplace are the source of the curriculum. This kind of curriculum is in contrast to more conventional university programmes that are usually organised around academically defined bodies of knowledge.

The chapter begins with a picture of the conceptual frame within which WBL programmes and portfolios are located. This picture includes a description of the institutional and programme context. This is followed by a discussion of the teaching and learning strategies involved in the writing of portfolios. Here we will draw attention to the particular kinds of identities that are being constructed through the pedagogical process. We will use examples of students' writing to examine some of the discursive shifts that are required as students construct a kind of autobiographical text that attempts to conflate personal, work and academic knowledges/selves.

This particular construction of self sits comfortably within an educational discourse that contributes to a naturalising of the relationship between learning and working. This relationship can be understood as contributing to, and symptomatic of, a deinstitutionalising of learning. We use the term 'deinstitutionalising' as a way of exploring the increasing legitimation of learning that occurs outside educational institutions – i.e. learning that occurs outside classrooms, at work and at leisure (McIntyre and Solomon 2000). However, at the same time, we do not wish to suggest that this deinstitutionalisation goes unchallenged. Indeed there are a number of challenges by educational institutions and these have a number of manifestations. The chapter examines one of these manifestations as universities work towards winning back learning through the introduction of new disciplinary practices that are contributing to the production of worker-learner subjects.

Writing about oneself as a pedagogical device is hardly an unfamiliar practice. Think of the place of diaries and learning journals that have been part and parcel of the pedagogical package of many educational programmes across all sectors. As discussed in Chapter 1 and as exemplified in the case studies in Chapters 4 and 8, the learning potential of this kind of reflective practice is a widely endorsed technology. Reflection texts are understood to be safe sites for articulating one's thoughts, reflections and experiences in a private space, a space that is seemingly unregulated. Usually there are no explicit genre rules to follow, no clear audience (other than oneself) and no correcting of the text. How you write and what you write is said to be 'up to you'. Nevertheless, in classrooms there is a pedagogical purpose behind the instruction to write a journal or diary and this is usually linked to a particular view of learning and learners – a view which brings together experience, reflection and learning.

Portfolios are also not new. For some time they have been a textual device for packaging an account of one's practices for a number of different purposes. They can include any number of things such as CVs, résumés, letters of reference and 'real' examples of work. More recently, the celebration of individualism in the new vocationalism portfolios, together with the rhetoric around the changing nature of work and workplaces, have given portfolios a new kind of legitimacy as a text for selling oneself for a job in a particular way (see Gee 2000). These are often named as 'career portfolios' and are said to provide evidence of an individual's knowledge and skills in working with information, people and things in a way that matches the desired kinds of workers (Wonacott 2001). Accompanying this way of presenting oneself for job-seeking purposes there is an increasing practice in higher and vocational education institutions that legitimates the use of portfolios for learning purposes, so as to enable non-traditional entry into educational programmes and to provide mechanisms that offer alternative modes of learning.

Portfolio development for learning purposes is the consideration of this chapter. Here we explore portfolio development as a pedagogical technology for both entry and learning purposes in WBL programmes.

In order to do this, we have chosen to examine portfolios as a type of narrative text, where the learners explicitly write their life story in a particular way. Theoretically, this exploration chooses to understand these texts as sites of identity formation. In relation to the narrative approach described in Chapter 3 we suggest that portfolios can be understood as sites where learners reflexively create a life story of themselves by drawing on available social and cultural resources. In the context of a university degree programme, the complexity of identifying and applying these resources cannot be underestimated. Such complexity comes to the fore when we consider answers to the following questions: What does a worker-learner look like? What does a worker-learner do? What kind of stories tell academics that a person is a worker-learner? Are these different stories to those told to colleagues or bosses, or recruiters in workplaces? Who will read these particular stories? Where else are such stories written or found? Who decides when a learner or a worker becomes a worker-learner? And on what basis? What is it in the story that indicates whether or not experience has become knowledge?

Modern policy, programmes and rhetoric concerning workers and 'lifelong learning' all assume that working and learning should be ongoing, and should be brought together. The questions just outlined make clear that this association or conflation is problematic. The 'worker-learner' is treated as if this is natural, or transparent, or an obvious identity, yet as our questions show the worker-learner is not so simple or obvious, or so easily produced.

In this chapter we have chosen to focus on the textual production of the worker-learner and the new kinds of learner identity work that this is producing. However, in doing so we do not want to diminish the significance of the teacher identity work that is complicit and implicit is this kind of pedagogical practice. Indeed, this pedagogy is located in a pedagogic site that is also a workplace, and academics (who are also workers) are discursively constructed as a new kind of working 'subject' – a kind that is symptomatic of the many challenges faced by academics as they position themselves (and find themselves positioned in) new relationships with organisations and different bodies of knowledge (Scheeres and Solomon 2000; Boud and Solomon 2001a).

Institutional site

Portfolio development is not confined to any one programme, nor to any one educational institution, and pedagogical practices vary considerably. Here it may be useful to provide some contextual information about this particular pedagogical site.

The university within which this programme is located is a recently formed technological university in Australia. Constituted as a university in 1988 its degree offerings and the identity of its academics have been shaped by quite a different history to those in the older universities in Australia. Specifically, its newness means that it has not been characterised by conventional disciplinary structures. While these exist at a macro-structure level, the university's image lies in its reputation for practice-based teaching. It describes itself as 'a new and progressive university, non-elitist and egalitarian, with a distinctive focus on professional practice' (Blake 2000). This focus has two significant manifestations. First, the university has strong partnerships, alignments and networks with industries and organisations in both the public and private sectors. Second, a high proportion of the student population is employed and studying part-time.

A third manifestation is in the way work and professional practices are integrated into almost all programmes at the university. Learners have many opportunities to use their work as a site of learning and as a learning resource. Professional placements, cooperative education arrangements and practica are available, and many learners are involved in action-learning projects and individual learning contracts in the workplace itself. The increased relationship between the academy and the workplace is now an everyday lived experience for many academics. Further, there is a recognition that learners bring to the learning situation a considerable amount of knowledge and experience that can count towards a degree. Therefore, prior learning is recognised and processes have been established for students to claim credit for work-related learning. In the main, these claims for recognition are made against existing learning outcomes articulated in subject and course documentation.

Pedagogical site

As indicated earlier, the pedagogical focus of this chapter is on a particular kind of programme that is relatively new. The programme is a set of WBL partnership postgraduate awards known as Professional Practice awards. These are an extension to existing programmes that in some shape or form already incorporate people's work and workplace as a site of learning. In Professional Practice awards an employee's work is the curriculum. In line with this, existing subjects or subject structures are not used to structure the curriculum. Rather the worker-learner is asked to write their own curriculum, by organising learning into a number of containers that enable them to reconstitute their work knowledge, experiences and practices as learning. The learning containers include work-based projects that focus on current or planned work, portfolios and the accompanying supporting statement texts that describe recently acquired knowledge.

A 'work as curriculum' pedagogical site has considerable appeal to potential worker-learners and their organisations. Many workers are asking for more 'relevant' learning and are seeking more qualifications and employment choices in situations where they have little time to participate in conventional academic learning. At the same time, organisations increasingly understand the importance of supporting learning practices at work in order to enhance organisational capability at a time of ongoing change and uncertainty. Moreover they are seeking to professionalise their workforce in order to be more competitive and retain their 'best' employees.

At the same time, universities are searching for new markets (i.e. income) with academics shifting the focus of their educational practices from teaching to learning. This broadening and changing of conventional approaches produces a number of challenges for all participants. While the university can provide a rationale for developing and delivering this kind of programme, numerous questions arise for both academics and learners. For example, how is learning at work counted? How is it measured? How are 'academic' standards maintained? And what effect does this have on the learning and the knowledge being produced?

These questions are complicated by the fact that in a WBL partnership, where work *is* the curriculum, individual learning programmes are often tied into the strategic goals of the participating organisation. This kind of curriculum is indeed a challenge to the university's view of the place of disciplinary knowledge. In WBL programmes the workplace, the individual learner and the university have to work together to produce and validate a non-disciplinary yet still legitimate knowledge.

This shift presents an unprecedented challenge to academics in terms of curriculum ownership and the balance of power and control. The conventional boundaries between theory and practice, between one discipline and another, between being a learner and a worker and between working and learning have become blurred and, not surprisingly, a site of contestation. Furthermore, while existing boundaries are being dismantled, *new and different kinds of boundaries are forming* – boundaries that frame the work-based curriculum and the identity of the worker-learner subject. In other words, the WBL curriculum does not lead to a disappearance of boundaries, it is not deregulated or unbounded, without any framing. Rather, the framing is different, local and specific, and certainly more complex, contested and fluid (Solomon and McIntyre 2000).

A large number of pedagogic and institutional interventions have been put into place to construct the new kind of worker-learner. While on the one hand the pedagogical practices acknowledge that work is a learning experience, on the other hand they also reveal that it is only by reconstituting work as a learning experience in institutional terms that it can be counted. This is one of the ways the university legitimises work and work practices as a source of knowledge that qualifies for a degree. In line with this, one of the key roles that the university has in the three-way partnership (university, workplace and employee) is the organisation of the learning programme into particular kinds of knowledge categories as well as having the sole responsibility for the assessment of each individual's learning.

Although the programme has been in place for several years, the complexities of this pedagogical practice have meant that the curriculum boundaries and the teaching and learning processes are under constant review. In a recent version at the macro-level, WBL comprises two stages: programme planning and programme implementation. Portfolio development takes place during the programme planning stage. In this stage of the WBL degree each learner negotiates a programme plan in consultation with his or her line manager and an academic adviser with the relevant content expertise. The programme plan comprises three assessment components: a proposal, a portfolio and a reflective essay. These components are submitted to the university for approval as an integrated WBL programme plan.

The proposal is organised around a number of areas of learning that correlate to the subjects in a conventional degree. These areas of learning are generated by each individual learner and take into account their existing skills, knowledge and understandings and their future learning needs. Some of these areas of learning correspond to the learner's claim for what is called 'recognition of current capability' (RCC) as demonstrated in the portfolio. Other areas focus on future learning which is organised around conventional university subjects and/or work-based projects.

RCC is a term that replaces the terms conventionally used in tertiary and higher education for the accreditation of learning that occurs outside educational institutions. In Australia the term is usually recognition of prior learning (RPL), while in the UK it is accreditation of prior and experiential learning (APEL). The use of the word 'current', in contrast to 'prior' draws attention to the need to make the learning contemporary. In other words, the learning experience has to be connected to one's current life and learning programme, rather than just something that happened at some prior point in one's life. The word 'capability', in contrast to 'learning' has resonance with language used in contemporary organisational discourses. By locating itself within organisational discourses, the term RCC draws attention to the product or knowledge resources that are the consequences of learning rather than focusing on the process of the learning itself.

Learning portfolio development

The portfolio provides a learner with the opportunity to present a case for the formal recognition and assignment of credit points for learning that demonstrates current capabilities. A claim of up to two-thirds of a degree can be made through the portfolio. The portfolio is also pedagogically presented as a mechanism that facilitates learners' understanding of the relationship between their work and learning. Therefore, the portfolio development process is understood as a device for developing capabilities that help the learner to respond actively to the combined learning requirements of the workplace and the university. These require an engagement with academic literacies and practices involved in the negotiation and writing of a WBL programme plan that meets degree requirements. In other words, learners need to translate their existing knowledge and experience into a form that counts in the university.

The formal mechanism for learner support in the development of their programmes consists of four day-long, face-to-face workshops staggered over 28 weeks. Academics design and present the workshop activities, which are organised around four processes, considered integral to planning a WBL programme:

- developing a conceptual understanding of your WBL degree
- developing a programme proposal
- providing evidence of prior learning through the development of a portfolio
- consolidating the components of your WBL programme plan.

These processes draw attention to a distinctive focus of this pro-gramme. Unlike in portfolio development subjects found in many educational institutions, in this site developing a portfolio is integral to a whole programme offering. Not only does it not stand alone as a discrete unit, but it also attempts to work with a way of learning and a form of knowledge that require a significant repositioning of both the curriculum and the learner. The processes and the accom-panying activities work with the idea that there is a relationship be-tween work experience and learning and therefore that being a worker means one is also a learner. However, while contemporary educa-tional discourses acknowledge that learners today do not always learn in classrooms, in order to be a worker who is also a learner in univer-sity terms the learning from work has to be articulated in particular textual performances. Worker-learners are not assessed or identified as such by their performance in conventional essays or exams. But neither do their work performances *per se* provide the right evidence or suggest that their learning at work is legitimate enough. Indeed, everyday work learning has to be turned into something else for it to be counted as learning by the university. In other words, the worker-learner has to write about (or translate) work in a way that can be understood in terms of academic discourse – however loose this category of knowledge has become.

In order to construct learning in a particular way and in order to produce a worker-learner, a number of teaching activities are em-ployed.[1] These are said to provide learners with the knowledge re-sources that will enable them to reconstitute their work practices and experiences into university understandings of knowledge.

One of these activities draws attention to the important role of reflection on learning (as described in Chapter 1). Here learners are asked to write a short reflection on what they have learnt from an experience at work. The following questions are offered as a guide:

- What did the experience involve?
- What do you think you learnt?
- What did it feel like?
- How has it changed the way you think about and do your work?
- Is there further related learning that you still need to do?

In other activities learners are encouraged to go beyond 'doing reflec-tion'. These activities work with reflection as an object of study (body of knowledge). They do so by mimicking, in a sense, more or less conventional kinds of academic student work. For example, learners are provided with guidance on ways of recognising different types of reflective writing. Based on Hatton and Smith's classifications (1995), three categories of writing are offered: descriptive writing; descriptive reflection; and critical (or dialogic) reflection. Learners are encouraged to understand the relationship between each type of writing and its context, purpose and audience. This is accompanied by a discussion of different theorists and their conceptions of reflection. The range of readings in the workbook includes selections from Anderson *et al.* (1998) 'Students' Guide to Learning Partnerships'; Binney and Williams (1997), *Learning into the Future: Changing the Way People Change Organizations*; Boud *et al.* (1985) *Reflection: Turning Experience into Learning*; and Senge (1990) *The Fifth Discipline: The Art and Practice of the Learning Organization.*

The learners' understanding of a link between learning and experience and the role of reflection in making this link is supported by other activities. One of these involves the questioning of a number of rather pedestrian clichés that have emerged in some of the experiential learning literature. These WBL learners are asked to discuss in groups each of the following statements:

- learning can be gained from positive and negative experiences;
- learning is dependent on the diversity of your experiences, not necessarily on the time spent on gaining the experience;
- learning that results from an experience may be unintentional;
- reflection on learning can be used to integrate quite disparate experiences.

The aim of activities such as these is to reposition the way learners think about the relationship between work and learning. They are intended to extend and open up understandings, but at the same time these openings are not without boundaries. Rather, they are tightly framed by a fixed structure and unnegotiable assessment tasks. Students are provided with explicit guidelines on how to write a portfolio and what is expected in terms of output. Importantly, throughout the workshop and the handbook activities, WBL learners are frequently reminded that the assessor of their portfolio is the key reader of their work. What is made clear is that these assessors are academics and their assessment will therefore be based on the educational (knowledge and writing) requirements of the university rather than the performance requirements of the participating organisation.

The portfolio text comprises three parts, each contributing to the construction of the worker-learner identity, as follows.

Curriculum vitae

The CV, as described in the manual, is a text that provides the assessor with a broad, chronological overview of the WBL learner's whole career, including brief descriptions of education, work and other relevant experience. Where relevant, these descriptions are to be cross-referenced to the areas of learning in the learner's RCC claim.

In terms of our interest in identity construction, the CV is an identity text that allows a person to temporally employ a continuous set of educational and work events in a more or less conventional western cultural form. It is a familiar text in that it closely resembles the CVs that are written by individuals as part of a recruitment or promotion process in professional job settings. The text constructs the person as an individual with a unique set of work and educational experiences. These experiences are written in a *when*, *where* and *what* format – a format that allows for a form of identification that is produced through a process of both individualisation and sameness.

Documentary evidence for each area of learning included in the RCC claim

This part of the portfolio, as described in the manual, is said to provide the assessor with formal and/or official evidence of the learning the learner has gained for each area of learning in their claim for RCC. This evidence can be direct (such as financial forecasts, work plans and training materials) or indirect (i.e. documents that conventionally signify the value of learning such as certificates, awards, references and evaluations).

These kinds of work documents are also texts that are connected to the identity formation of the WBL learner. While these documents have not been specifically constructed for this WBL programme, by bringing them into the learning discursive domain they nevertheless become part of the personal narrative of the WBL learner. By selecting certain kinds of documentary evidence the learner is actively making decisions about which bits of text (evidence) have contributed to their *being* in this particular context.

Supporting statements for each area of learning included in the RCC claim

The supporting statements, as described in the manual, are considered to be the most important part of the portfolio. They are said to be the site that provides the assessor with a strong case demonstrating the achievement of the learning outcomes for each of the areas of learning in the learner's claim for RCC. They also link each of the three parts of the portfolio together in that they elaborate on key learning experiences outlined in the CV and explain the documentary evidence.

The workshops stress the point that it is not enough to include documentary evidence in the portfolio. The argument is that while documents do provide evidence of 'successful' learning or working within particular contexts at a particular time, as stand alones they do not provide the necessary supporting story that can connect the various working or learning experiences. Nor can these documents be considered to be legitimate within the available academic discourses that inform decisions on whether or not learning can count as academic learning. In other words, the message is that documentary evidence has little value in academic terms in this programme. In order to count a story needs to be written around the documents in order to construct a particular kind of storyteller/identity. This storyteller is a person who has not only worked and learnt in the past but is a person who is able to reflexively construct their identity through a process of self-narration. And in creating this life story the person needs to demonstrate that they can draw on available social and cultural resources that have currency within the academy.

Pedagogical advice is provided to help the WBL learners find a different way of identifying themselves. For example, they are asked to explain why particular evidence has been chosen, its relevance and in what ways it demonstrates their capability in the specified area of learning. The site for this explanation is in these supporting statements. When writing their supporting statements WBL learners are told that for particular work experiences to count they must go beyond a statement of their performance – i.e. what they have done or how they have done it. They are told to discuss what they have learnt and the ways in which the learning has been applied to work. Implicit within this advice is the fact that accounts of knowledge and work practices in themselves do not count, but understanding what knowledge has been gained and articulation of the application of this new knowledge does.

In order to help learners to see that the evidence does not 'speak for itself' each is asked to bring a piece of evidence that they plan to use in their portfolio claim. In groups they focus on one person's evidence. In the first part of the activity, all group members (including the person whose evidence it is) write down what they think can be assumed about the learning achieved from the evidence as it stands. In the second part of the activity, group members are encouraged to ask the person whose evidence it is to provide the group with information about the learning which the evidence demonstrates. One person in the group acts as the scribe, writing out the questions the group asks. Following this activity the questions are discussed as is any discrepancy between the assumptions made by the person providing the evidence and other members of the group. The learners are reminded that the assessor would be in a very similar position to other members of the group who in many cases could ascertain very little about the learning that the evidence showed without the further explanation gained by the group on asking key questions. This leads into a discussion of the role of the supporting statements in the portfolio.

Learners are required to develop a supporting statement for each of the areas of learning in their claim for RCC. The supporting statements form the site for the argument they present to convince the assessor that they have an understanding of each of the learning outcomes for the areas of learning in their RCC claim. To further explain the purpose of the supporting statements, learners are provided with an analogy of a lawyer presenting a case. This analogy draws attention to the way certain kinds of evidence cannot stand alone. The strength of the case is built around how convincingly the lawyer can explain the relevance of the evidence in demonstrating his or her argument.

Textualising the worker-learner: some examples

As illustrated above, the textual work of the worker-learner is complicated. It involves the construction of three narratives: a CV; a selection of official documents; and a number of supporting statements. Each of these narratives produces a different but related dimension of the identity of the worker-learner. The CV does this by providing a historical profile of their work and education experiences. The selected documents provide an external 'authenticity' to their work and education experiences, while the support statements are the exposition site that legitimises their work and educational experiences in more conventional academic terms.

The writing of the supporting statements is the most challenging element. The writing of the CV and the selection of documents are familiar textual activities in professional situations. However, the genre of supporting statements is an unfamiliar and consequently confusing one. Its complexity lies in the way it requires the learner, through their writing, to position themselves and their work in a way that produces a hybrid worker-learner text and thus identity. This hybrid text exemplifies and produces a boundary crossing between professional and academic domains and between being a worker and being a learner in a higher education institution.

In supporting statements the identity of the worker-learner – the 'I' in the narrative – is not constructed as a 'doer', but as a person who sits back and critically reviews their work and learning. And the reviews of these work and learning activities are not presented as discrete ones but are articulated as resources for developing a set of capabilities that speaks to academics. In this text what is at stake is how the writers position themselves in relation to their knowledge. What is required is a cohesive argument that both individualises and generalises and as such resembles, but is not the same as, expositions found in other academic learning situations.

The complexity of this task is manifest in many of the initial drafts of the learners.[2] Often they comprise a more or less conventional recount of work and/or learning activities, thematised with 'I'. Some first draft examples are 'I attended a workshop . . .'; 'I provided an extensive advisory service to . . .'; 'I responded to inquiries . . .'; 'I wrote training manuals . . .'.

Other similarly less 'successful' supporting statements are written in conversational language as personal reflections on an aspect of a worker's professional practice. One example is:

> I have become very concerned about the way in which a diag-
> nosis can lead a parent down a particular road of support that
> may or may not be useful in their endeavours to help their
> child. Once a 'learning disability' label is given, some teachers are
> quick to install panic in parents and make alarm bells ring for
> them.

The following extract from a supporting statement, on the other hand, demonstrates (perhaps more successfully) how another learner is learning to textually represent herself as a person who is doing identity work in an appropriate way:

> My experience with the implementation of national competency based qualification, necessitated the development of a learning team working under very tight time constraints, and similarly provided an opportunity to reflect on the factors which supported our best outcomes and those which mitigated against them. This project provided me with valuable skills and knowledge in managing action learning within a wholly new externally directed framework. The stresses of responding rapidly to organisational imperatives within uncertain guidelines and with few system supports were extremely wearing on the team. This situation demanded an extension of my mediation and team building skills, and a capacity to clarify project dimensions and expectations with a wide range of stakeholders. Through meeting very tough deadlines, and reflecting with the team on the outcomes, I gained a new understanding of the importance of developing a shared sense of purpose, while encouraging an open agenda for critical evaluation and personal goal setting.

An analysis of this text reveals a different positioning of the narrator to the narrative being produced. This comes through in a number of ways. For example, the narrative does not read like a recount and the narrator, while still visible, is not always articulated through 'I' statements. The worker and the nature of the work practices are evident but these have been translated into a language that abstracts the worker and the actions into a form of knowledge that speaks to academic readers. It is in a language that is familiar and can be understood as academic discourse. This can be seen in the way the grammar has moved the information from 'doing' processes (action verbs) to a packaging of clauses where the meanings come through the use of lexically dense noun groups (e.g. 'a wholly new externally directed framework' and 'an extension of my mediation and team building skills'). Furthermore the key vocabulary items (i.e. the nouns and verbs) are drawn from two fields of knowledge – the professional field (e.g. 'responding rapidly to organisational imperatives') and the learning or educational one (e.g. 'gained a new understanding of . . . critical evaluation'). Presenting the two fields together produces hybridity, and thus a sign to the academic assessor that the writer is positioning themselves as a worker-learner.

A dimension of the pedagogical process and assessment requirement in the first stage of the programme is the writing of a reflection
essay. The intention of this essay is to mirror the learning processes
that are integral to the design of a WBL programme. In other words,
the learners are encouraged to note throughout the process the various struggles and challenges they experience in engaging with this
new way of academic learning.

However, these essays also provide insights into the struggles and
complexities of the identity work involved in the writing of both a
WBL programme and the accompanying portfolio. This section will
close with some extracts taken from one such essay written by one of
the master-level students. She is responsible for vocational education
in community services in the technical and further education system
for the state of New South Wales, Australia. Interestingly, in her
essay the student asks questions about knowledge and learning that
resemble many of the questions that academics themselves are also
asking.

> What are these glimpses of attraction, depth and possibility that
> entice me to stay? I am developing knowledge. What is that knowl-
> edge? How could it be characterised? What are the gaps? How
> well do the theories fit? Can I myself build any new ways of
> seeing?
>
> I go back to ask what my partner, the university, is seeking in
> me. I read the characteristics of masters degree learning and find
> them very confronting (Work Based Learning Program Planning
> Workbook: 67). Am I really an independent knowledge builder?
> Can I theorise and generalise? Will others find my work useful?
> Has this partner over-estimated my potential?
>
> In this survey of what I need to be able to do in my learning
> partnership, I see that some of the characteristics look familiar
> and easy. For example, I know how to plan complex projects
> involving lots of resources and including the work of others. In
> fact, that kind of synthesis of combined efforts toward a goal is
> one of my pleasures and talents. I know how to apply learning in
> diverse and uncertain contexts – and have spent much of the past
> three years helping others to do that with me. And I am also
> quite creative in choosing appropriate communication media, and
> ensuring that my way of responding to new situations is adaptive.
>
> But some of the other characteristics of masters' level learning
> look much more challenging and new. The ability to formulate

theoretical concepts with explanatory value, to apply a reasoned methodology, to evaluate ideas using critical analysis and synthesis resulting in an original contribution to knowledge – these expectations look far more scary. When I look more closely at these characteristics they throw light on the delayed commitment! I find some clues in the fact that the disciplines of managing projects and their outcomes are much more familiar to me than the disciplines of managing the resultant thinking and knowledge. This emphasis on 'the practical over the theoretical . . . and contextualised knowledge over generalisable knowledge' (McIntyre *et al.* 1999: 11) is a recognised feature of the professional identity of vocational teachers and was a key issue in my long program-planning process – my initial plan identified what I had done, and what I would do, rather than how I would think and what I (and others) would learn from my work.

On finding that I may not yet have all the qualities my new partner relies on, I am thrown back on trust. Will the university have the interest, the time, the energy to work on these things with me? Or will it sail off on new voyages of discovery, hoping to come back to find me thriving and productive? How will I gain the skills? Can I keep my new partner interested for long enough to gain ground for a more equal relationship?

Her concluding remarks reveal the identity work that has been taking place during the programme and portfolio development process:

The process has required the slow development of a new self-image as a student. This identity is still shaky, as the amount of time available and depth of study possible lead to a limited engagement and I often feel like a poor approximation to a postgraduate student. At other times, however, as when presenting to the sponsoring committee the results of a research project at work, I see the fruits of my reading and thinking – and know that I am approaching work from a different and wider reflective framework.

As a result, I realise, that while it may seem to me that I've been only flirting with this new partnership, I've been irretrievably changed by the encounter. I've already learned more than I realised, and developed new ways of thinking about the construction of knowledge. In my reflective learning processes I begin to name my learning. I am developing my capacity to theorise my work.

This is a learning process – feeling my way into the territory opened up by this new relationship. It requires a very independent approach. It will be interesting to see where it takes me.

Concluding comments

In this chapter we have looked at identity construction through an examination of the pedagogical practices involved in the development of portfolios in a higher education WBL programme. Our focus has been on the textual practices, suggesting that these are an interesting pedagogical site to explore the way learners produce themselves as worker-learners. In doing so we have revealed a number of complexities around this identity construction – complexities that problematise the idea that this kind of identity is transparent and easily produced.

To return to one of the key questions asked at the beginning of the chapter – What does a worker-learner look like? – it seems that in the context of a WBL programme in textual terms a worker-learner can be understood as a person who is able to write a particular kind of narrative. This narrative is one where they position themselves in a way that both personalises and abstracts their work and learning experiences. Arguably in doing so they demonstrate that they have learnt about the relationship between work and learning, and between learning and experience, and the relationship between professional and academic writing.

We suggest that the realisation of these intersecting relationships is accompanied by a number of struggles around what counts as knowledge and what counts as this new kind of being. As suggested in this chapter there is no single or simple definition of what such struggles mean in university terms. Rather, as academics we have taken a view that these constructions will continue to be contested ones and that the pedagogical practices attached to WBL programmes can not only be understood as learner identity struggles but also as identity struggles for academics and for the institution itself.

Notes

1 All activities in this chapter are described in the *Program Planning Workbook*, Faculty of Business, University of Technology, Sydney (2000).
2 These examples come from edited drafts of the work of students enrolled in a Master of Professional Practice in Education.

Chapter 6

Pedagogy as a tool for corporate culture

Working for oneself

Introduction

In the early 1980s, culture entered the lexicon of organisations. With the development and popularisation of the concept of 'corporate culture', starting largely with Peters and Waterman's massively successful book *In Search of Excellence* (1982), what was formerly a relatively unknown notion has now become part of the everyday discourse of organisations from the shop floor to the boardroom. Spawning a plethora of both popular texts and academic treatises, organisational and corporate culture have come of age as a means to understand, manage and change organisational behaviour. Indeed, the situation is now one where 'culture' is accorded a prime position in terms of how contemporary organisational life is governed (du Gay 1996a), and for senior executives culture is now most commonly understood as a lever that can be pulled in order to enhance organisational performance. For many businesses this has meant a preoccupation with 'the consideration of culture and emotions as decisive factors influencing both individual behaviour and enterprise results' (Ibarra-Colado 2002: 165). Further, these changes in the government of organisational lives are significant in terms of their potential effects on the personal identity of those at work (du Gay 1996b).

With culture having grown as an important construct for the management of organisations, so too have technologies that are designed to change culture. Not the least of these are pedagogical practices that seek to influence individual behaviour and self-image in a way that is said to be supportive of an organisation's goals and facilitative of the development of managerially defined and preferred culture. These new practices, most often developed and implemented by consulting firms, mark a significant departure from the more conventional approaches to skills-based and vocational training that have traditionally dominated organisational investment in education. This departure is one where the pedagogical goal is explicitly stated as being to change the very nature of who people (in this case employees) are. Such changes are also related to the growth of self-help literature discussed in Chapter 4 – for example, the ideas of self-help writers such as Stephen Covey are also used in corporate contexts.

In the light of these changes, this chapter will explore the 'pedagogies of the self' that are employed by cultural change programmes in organisations. In order to do so, two case studies will be examined. The first will be Landmark Education Business Development Inc.'s (LEBD) transformational change programme. This programme is designed to create leadership and commitment among an organisation's workforce and, as a result, to 'produce sustainable change and unprecedented business results' (LEBD 2002). For Landmark, such results are said to be achieved through the full involvement, participation and commitment of employees in that 'stimulating people to act in new ways and giving them the power to do so is one of the most important differences between those companies that stagnate and those that develop and sustain a competitive edge' (LEBD 2002). The second case study will be McKinsey and Co.'s 'cultural capital' approach. This approach 'focuses on building a high-performance organisation by liberating the personal' (Trinca 2001). Such liberation is linked to 'bringing meaning back into people's lives in business' (Rennie in Kohn 2000) in a way that individual and business needs can be aligned. As a pedagogical intervention, the McKinsey approach involves lengthy training programmes on trust, self-awareness and communication in order to bring a 'spiritual quotient' into work and to infuse work with meaning.

For the purpose of this chapter, information regarding Landmark and McKinsey's programmes and methodology was all gathered from publicly available sources. In the case of Landmark this included descriptions of the programme available from LEBD's own marketing materials (Landmark Education 2001; LEBD 2002) and more academically oriented papers on Landmark's educational philosophy and methodology, written or co-authored by Landmark personnel (Marzano *et al.* 1995; McCarl *et al.* 2001). This was supplemented by business school cases on LEBD published by the Harvard Business School (Wruck and Eastley 1998) and the University of California's Marshall Business School (Logan 1998), as well as an investigative report of Landmark published in the magazine *Sales and Marketing Management* (Marchetti 1999). In the case of McKinsey, information was gathered from the wide coverage McKinsey has had in the

Australian press, particularly the business paper *The Australian Financial Review* (Fox and Trinca 2001; Pheasant 2001; Trinca 2001; Cave 2002) and the transcript of a radio talk show on spirituality in business in which McKinsey partner David Rennie participated (Kohn 2000). Further sources from the media included the *Wall Street Journal* (Voigt 2002) and *Business Review Weekly* (Treadgold 2002). Discussions of McKinsey's programmes in the web-based *Business Spirit Journal Online* (Feasey 2002; Hutner 2002) were also consulted. Together these materials provided a wealth of information on the processes and methodologies of the programmes run by each of the companies and allowed us to reflect on the programmes to discuss more generally the relationship between corporate culture, pedagogy and employee identity.

The chapter begins with an introduction to the emergence of corporate culture as a relatively new approach to understanding and managing organisations. This is followed by a description of the pedagogical approaches used by Landmark and McKinsey to facilitate changes in the culture of organisations. We then reflect on these case studies in terms of how they construct and attempt to modify identity in a way that subsumes that identity within a corporate discourse. In particular, we discuss how pedagogies of corporate culture propose that employees adopt particular types of selves that, described as being 'authentic' or 'true' selves, are unproblematically said to be directly related to commercial success within a capitalist framework. Indeed, we suggest that it is this de-complexified conflation of humanism and capitalism that informs the pedagogy of corporate culture. The chapter concludes with a discussion of the implication of the pedagogies of corporate culture and identity for the dialogic relationship people have with their work.

Culture and identity

Part of the appeal and popularity of the notion of corporate culture is that it enables managers to think about and act upon the less formal aspects of organisations. It purports to discover and manage what lies 'underneath the rational-technical veneer of business' (Deal and Kennedy 1999: 1). In turn, the management of culture is most commonly based on the desire to produce strong and consistent cultures where the behaviour of individual employees is informed by a managerially sanctioned common set of values, behaviours and assumptions across the organisation. Alvesson and Berg (1992)

critically enumerate a number of reasons that are used to justify this
desire:

- a strong culture leads to competitive advantage as it enables
  people to identify with the company so as to be a source of
  individual commitment;
- a strong culture provides an advanced form of managerial control directed at people's values, beliefs and ideologies;
- a strong culture enables organisations to better use their human
  resources by tapping into their unexploited human potential;
- implementing cultural change enables managers to align individual
  behaviour with corporate strategy.

What is assumed in this is the close relationship between collective
and individual identities, as a singular corporate culture is intended
to directly influence the behaviour of individuals. The identity of
people at work is therefore brought into question; identity is seen as
something that organisations and their managers have at their disposal such that it can be changed and aligned with corporate imperatives in order to produce improved organisational performance. It is
in this way that the concept of culture can be represented as a 'tool
that mediates and intervenes the organizing process' (Chan 2000:
21). Thus, culture is a governmental technique used to develop particular relationships to self by members of an organisation – culture
is 'intimately bound up with questions of identity' (du Gay 1996a:
152). This 'binding up' is based on governing the behaviour of individuals in organisations by proposing to fabricate new identities for
them 'as subjects of excellence, making them directly accountable for
the fate of the organization' (Ibarra-Colado 2002: 173).

Within the literature on organisational and corporate culture there
is a variety of definitions and explanations of culture. Arguably,
however, these definitions have in common 'the view that culture
consists of some combination of artefacts (also called practices,
expressive symbols, or forms), values and beliefs, and underlying
assumptions that organizational members *share* about appropriate
behaviour' (Detert *et al.* 2000: 851). This relationship is said to be
such that culture is generated through beliefs and values that are
commonly held among members of the organisation; these in turn
are expressed through artefacts, structures and behaviours (Harris
and Ogbona 2002). The basis of culture is thus posited as shared
forms of identity (in the form of assumptions, values and beliefs) that

inform a common approach to behaviour in organisations. Indeed it is its 'shared' nature that is the key to understanding how corporate culture is conceived, such that 'corporate culture protagonists have promised managers that it is possible to manage culture in order to improve social integration and commitment in the organization, thereby ultimately gaining innovativeness, productivity and competitive advantage' (Dahler-Larsen 1994: 1). Thus, to change culture is a process through which the values and beliefs of employees must be changed and where the diversity of possible identities that people bring to their organisation are shepherded into the confines of an assumed commonality. On this basis, organisations are said to be able to implement culture change programmes that attempt to instil a new form of shared identity among their employees – a form that better enables the organisation to achieve its goals. These goals, while potentially different between organisations, are invariably defined in commercial terms such as competitive differentiation, cost management, customer services, profitability and brand differentiation (Harris and Ogbona 2002).

Although there are a diversity of academic arguments concerning the nature of organisational culture and its manageability, in organisations themselves the concept of culture has serious currency and directly influences managerial and organisational behaviour. The promise that such an approach makes is that culture can be 'managed' – it suggests an instrumental perspective that focuses on the purposive, rational aspects of culture to create a climate that fosters particular attitudes and desired behaviours that promote and enable particular organisational strategies (Alvesson and Berg 1992). Such culturalism is 'the answer to a manager's prayer – a way to solve the problems of their organization by manipulating the beliefs, rituals and language of their employees' (Parker 2000: 2). It therefore becomes incumbent on managers to design programmes and implement techniques that enable culture to be changed. Such change programmes, more often than not, 'share the common fundamental aims of the reorganization of the workplace and the production of new sets of attitudes, beliefs and behavior among corporate employees to enable increased productivity and profitability for the organization' (Casey 1999: 156). Thus an advocacy of corporate culture proposes that 'an organization that can effectively manage its culture has gone a long way towards effective management' (Denton 1998: 175) and that 'the only thing of real importance that leaders do is to create and manage culture' (Schein 1992: 5).

If culture change is important, then managers must ask themselves what practices they have at their disposal to create such changes. These practices include manipulation of reward and recognition systems, promotion criteria, performance management processes, organisational structure, recruitment communication and so forth. Such practices are often implemented though 'constant driven reform initiatives for corporations to gain control of their organizations through influencing the value premises on which organizational members' behaviors are based' (Chan 2000: 12). Important here is the idea that culture is not a vague and unmanageable concept, but rather that 'the culture of the business enterprise is only operationalized through particular practices and technologies . . . through which senior managers . . . seek to delineate, normalize and instrumentalize the conduct of persons in order to achieve the ends that they postulate as desirable' (du Gay 1996a: 61). In terms of the subject matter of this chapter, therefore, we seek to understand this process specifically in terms of pedagogical practices and technologies. We suggest that these technologies actively seek to 'contribute to the deliberate fashioning of employee identities by appropriating identities within the language of empowerment, belonging, reward and valuing individual difference' (Garrick and Solomon 2001: 301). One such technology that has emerged as an important tool for organisational change is the formal training programme designed to align people to preferred corporate cultures. It is a discussion of such programmes as they relate to worker identity that forms the basis of the remainder of this chapter.

Landmark education: realising one's transcendental consciousness

The Landmark Education Corporation was founded in 1991 when Werner Erhard and Associates was purchased by a group of former employees. This entitled the new organisation to use the intellectual property associated with the training programmes created during the 1970s and 1980s by Walter Erhard (Wruck and Eastley 1998). Based on Erhard's 'technology', Landmark developed Erhard's original approach into the Landmark Forum – a short training course claiming to offer personal growth and transformation. The Landmark Forum proposes that it can create a 'breakthrough in living . . . a means of gaining insight into fundamental premises that shape and govern our lives – the very structures that determine our thinking, our actions, our values, the kind of people that we can be' (Landmark Education

2001: 1). For participants this means 'examining the basis of your identity, your personality, your formulas for living, relating and achieving success' (2001: 3). The results of this self-examination are stated as being:

- you expand your effectiveness and deepen your satisfaction in the most basic areas of life;
- you break through the confines of even the best conventional thinking . . . to step beyond the limits of your identity;
- you infuse daily commitments and routines with a new spirit;
- you achieve a marked increase in productivity;
- you gain clarity about your priorities and values (2001: 3).

From these beginnings in 1991, Landmark has expanded to over 90 locations around the world. Significant to our discussion here, in 1994 LEBD was formed as a wholly owned subsidiary of Landmark Education Corporation, set up to offer 'custom designed programs to transform an organization's culture' (Wruck and Eastley 1998: 14).

Landmark makes significant claims for the benefits of their programmes. Steve Zaffron, president of LEBD suggests:

> Corporate culture change experts and scholars report that transforming corporate culture takes years and needs an army of consultants . . . [but] a central premise of our work is that the individuals in an enterprise and the enterprise itself, have the possibility not only of fulfilment and success, but also of greatness.
>
> (Zaffron cited in Logan 1998)

In making this claim, LEBD takes Erhard's original 'technology' and applies it to the redesign of an organisation's culture and practices. Zaffron explains this as follows:

> We see an organization as a network of conversations. Our work is based on the paradigm that people's behaviour is a function of conversation – how they see the world and how they talk about it to themselves and others. We can talk about motivation and all the rest, but when push comes to shove, behavior is really a function of how people see things.
>
> (LEBD 2002)

In organisations these 'conversations' are said to operate at three levels, and Landmark offer interventions at each of these levels. The executive level conversations focus on corporate strategy and are addressed by Landmark's strategic planning process; the operational level conversations are concerned with projects for change and are supported by teams of employees coached by Landmark employees; and the individual level conversations are addressed by a three and a half day workshop (Wruck and Eastley 1998). Thus, Landmark suggest that they gain access to an organisation's culture by viewing the organisation as a network of conversations and that by improving the way people participate in these conversations people will change the way they view their work, and change their actions so as to produce improved organisational results (Logan 1998).

The workshops that are used to change the conversations of individual employees are designed to be transformational in nature. For example, as reported by Logan (1998), in the mid-1990s Landmark implemented their programme at BHP New Zealand – New Zealand's only fully integrated steel maker and largest steel producer. As part of the programme, the entire workforce was invited to attend a three and a half day workshop entitled 'Leadership for Inventing the Future' (LFIF). The programme was designed to enable employees to focus inquiry into the nature of their work, rethink what was possible for the organisation and for themselves, and to participate in a dialogue to develop new levels of commitment and performance at work. The 'bottom line promise' to participants was that 'you will transform who you are *being* at work' (Logan 1998: 6, emphasis added). Logan (1998: 19–20) outlines the content of the programme, which included:

- 'Identifying fundamental concerns that unawaredly [sic] affect and impact the way people speak and listen'
- 'Distinguishing the nature of language and its impact on the life and world of people at work'
- 'Distinguishing the conversations that make up the culture of New Zealand Steel'
- 'Learning to determine the facts of a situation independent from one's personal interpretation'
- 'Distinguishing "authenticity" in such a way as to allow new levels of self-expression and performance'
- 'Providing access to new ways of being and relating to others at work that go beyond past successes'
- 'Continuing to provide access to new ways of being at work which transcend ways of being from the past'
- 'Create projects to produce extraordinary results'

- 'Individuals declaring new possibilities for themselves at work and generating new commitments for what they are up to in the organization and individuals committing to specific results as an expression of those new commitments'.

Landmark claims that the methodology that enables them to realise the transformational goals of their programmes is based on a practical philosophy; indeed, their programmes explicitly recognise the contribution of philosophers as diverse as Aristotle, Albert Camus, Jurgen Habermas, Martin Heidegger, Immanuel Kant, Plato, Jean-Paul Sartre, Socrates, Charles Taylor and Ludwig Wittgenstein (Wruck and Eastley 1998). Their programmes have been described as a 'contemporary experience of Socratic philosophy in the making' (McCarl *et al.* 2001) as they extol the virtues of self-knowledge as the road to new action and practical wisdom. The programmes are also said to 'challenge conventional thinking, discursively examine the nature of human nature, and facilitate participants' exploration of their lives' (McCarl *et al.* 2001: 51). In terms of their corporate programmes, Landmark claim that this personal wisdom is directly and causally linked to business success – this suggests that 'stimulating people to act and giving them the power to do so may be the singular most important difference between those companies that stagnate and those that develop a competitive edge' (LEBD 2002).

The reasoning that informs Landmark's promise of person and business transformation is the notion that they offer 'non-traditional education . . . we shine a light on a dark place. We take off the blinders' (Landmark quoted in Marchetti 1999: 58). This is achieved by the facilitation of what Landmark call 'second-order change'. Such a change is said to address and change existing frameworks of perception and belief rather than just operating within them – or, as they put it, creating an ontological rather than a psychological change (Marzano *et al.* 1995). In a reading of Kuhn, they suggest that a paradigm is a set of beliefs that help a person make sense of the world and that 'shared paradigms are the very fabric of culture' (Marzano *et al.* 1995: 164). In turn by defining ontology as 'the study of the basic assumptions which underpin our paradigms' they propose that ontological change can be achieved by allowing individuals to 'experience their paradigms as constructed realities rather than absolute reality, and . . . experience . . . consciousness other than the "I" embedded in their paradigms'. In terms of identity this proposes that people define themselves as an 'I' within their paradigms, but that there is 'a self separate from the "I" of our thinking' – a 'transcendental consciousness'. Second order change is then said to occur when people develop a commitment to new paradigms that are 'consciously selected as opposed to culturally or situationally imposed', such that a person can engage in 'authentic speaking and listening . . . [by] taking possession of one's self *as one is*' (Marzano *et al.* 1995: 165, 167, 168, 169). Thus by changing people's collective paradigms in order for them to take possession of their true selves and consciously select the most effective paradigm, organisations can mobilise their cultures to achieve breakthrough results.

McKinsey and Co.: spirituality and cultural capital

McKinsey and Co. is one of the largest and perhaps most prestigious consulting companies in the world. The firm is said to be 'the high priest of high-level consulting, with the most formidable intellectual firepower, the classiest client portfolio, and the greatest global reach of any adviser to management in the world' (Byrne 2002: 66). Focused on corporate-based management consulting, their work consists mainly of providing advice to large corporations on issues of corporate strategy and performance. In line with this managerial focus, more recently McKinsey has developed a range of leadership and motivation interventions for organisations based on concepts such as 'emotional intelligence', 'spiritualty quotient' and 'cultural capital'. Working both with managerial and non-managerial employees, McKinsey engages with its clients to implement a series of activities including diagnostic tools to assess corporate culture, and workshops and training sessions designed to focus people on developing their 'selves' within the context of the organisations they work for. A key element of this is 'spirituality'-based training programmes to help people get in touch with their values, identity and purpose in life, which is said to raise the consciousness of the organisation. Further, what the McKinsey approach proposes is that by raising the consciousness of people at work, profits will also increase (Rennie and Bellin 1999).

In relation to corporate culture, the McKinsey approach is to create cultural change by focusing on individual employees and their relationship with the organisations where they work. For example, working with large Australian corporations such as Woodside Energy and the ANZ Bank, McKinsey has focused on 'building a

high performance organisation by liberating the personal to encourage the development of "cultural capital" ' (Fox and Trinca 2001).
The development of this service has been led by the Australian based
director of McKinsey, Michael Rennie. Rennie's decision to pursue
this work for McKinsey has been linked to his own life experience.
He was diagnosed with cancer at the age of 31 and is said to have
beaten his illness through a combination of chemotherapy and a 'pas-
sionate belief in the power of the mind to manufacture white blood
cells' (Trinca 2001). Following his recovery, Rennie employed his
new found beliefs in the power of the self to develop the new service
line for McKinsey, 'where values, spirit, cultural capital and meaning
are as important as the bottom line cost containment and corporate
strategy' (Trinca 2001). This approach draws much from the conventional psychology of Abraham Maslow by suggesting that self-
actualisation is the highest form of personal need. Further, by going
beyond a 'rationalist' approach to management, it suggests that bringing 'emotional intelligence' into the workforce can create a trusting
and 'co-creative' corporate culture (Pheasant 2001). This culture also
contains what Rennie calls the 'spiritual quotient' – the ability for
people to become emotionally engaged in their work and to feel that
they are making a difference (Cave 2002).

What this suggests is that in order to maximise employee motivation, people should be allowed to 'be themselves' at work. As Rennie
has explained, 'business serves us well in some ways, but it doesn't
serve us as fully as it could; it doesn't serve us fully as people. We put
on masks when we come into the workplace and that doesn't serve
us' (cited in Trinca 2001). This notion of 'allowing people to be
themselves' is central to the overall approach McKinsey takes (and
readers might like to compare this approach with that of the self-help
books discussed in Chapter 4, also ostensibly aiming to rediscover
the authentic self; the worker-learner training discussed in Chapter 5,
which 'textually' constructs a particular form of self; and the programmes to 'interrupt' gendered identity and renovate the self discussed in Chapter 8). Thus, it is proposed that organisations
increasingly need to ensure that their employees bring their 'selves'
fully to work. Explaining this, Rennie has proposed that in the Industrial Revolution people were required only to bring their bodies to
work, that in the information revolution people were required to
bring their intellect to work, and that today's requirement for creativity at work requires people to bring their 'emotional selves' to
work (Kohn 2000). McKinsey also suggests that people need to focus

on their spiritual selves such that meaning is brought back to work – this is said to be nothing less that 'a historic moment where what people want and what businesses want is finally coming together after centuries of it being separated' (Rennie cited in Kohn 2000).

Pedagogically, McKinsey's approach employs a number of techniques that are designed to increase the consciousness and self-actualisation of employees. These techniques are implemented through extensive change management workshops where, for example, 25 employees assemble for between two and four days to work on issues related to trust, self-awareness and communication (Trinca 2001). In one case, one of McKinsey's clients also ran workshops for the spouses and adult children of employees so that they could be exposed to the ideas and not be 'left out' of the experience. Specific pedagogical tools employed in these workshops include:

- **Reflection time and meditation.** Employees are led through a series of reflective exercises and encouraged to meditate. The focus of this reflection is to develop a 'culture of creativity' and a clearer sense of where they are going as individuals and what makes them 'happy'. The idea behind this is to enable people to reach their full potential and to 'bring all of their self to work' (Feasey 2002).
- **Visualisation.** Transformational techniques designed to help move people's work focus from their 'heads to their hearts' (Hutner 2002).
- **360-degree feedback.** A review and reflection of survey results where peers, reports and managers are asked to rate each participant's workplace behaviour (Trinca 2001).
- **Emotional quotient.** A review of participants' experience of change based on Daniel Goleman's (1996) notion of 'emotional intelligence' (Trinca 2001).
- **'Clearing'.** A technique where employees are taught to 'clear' (say what is on their mind) prior to discussing formal agenda items in meetings (Trinca 2001).

McKinsey proposes that their approach not only develops individuals but also leads to significant financial results. For example, it is claimed that by implementing the programmes in a large telecommunications company, the organisation saw a 65 per cent reduction in staff turnover within four months; another example claims productivity increases of 400 per cent (Hutner 2002). This highlights the justification that corporate investment in 'spirituality' programmes is good business as it can boost productivity and efficiency. In the words of Rennie: 'what's good for the spirit is good for the bottom line' (cited in Voigt 2002). The relationship between spirituality and financial performance is said to be based on the idea that if people have a clearer notion of who they are and the spiritual purpose behind what they are doing, they will focus more strongly. It is here that McKinsey's approach directly links notions of identity with its interventions into the workplace: 'corporate transformation is individual transformation; whatever it is you're wanting to transform or shift, you've actually got to shift the individuals, because at the end of the day it comes down to that' (Rennie cited in Kohn 2000).

The impossible promise of corporate culture

Whereas the previous two sections of this chapter have sought to provide an overview of the pedagogical approaches used by Landmark and McKinsey, we now reflect on these cases in order to provide an interpretation of them in terms of how they implicitly and explicitly relate pedagogy to identity. Our review is not intended as an evaluation of the effects of the programmes on particular people who have participated in them (many of whom report significant personal benefits), but rather as a critical reading of some of the pedagogical implications of the programmes. Arguably, the types of pedagogical practices that are used in the cultural change programmes that we have described here are designed to produce particular types of people by positioning them as humanistic autonomous selves whose identity is contextualised organisationally. In relation to our earlier discussion in Chapter 3, such pedagogies attempt to relay a particular relational narrative that stakes a claim in determining the lives of members of organisations – a narrative that they must interact with in order to survive. Thus, corporate culture presents a model of being at work, and the associated pedagogies work to encourage people to reflexively use this narrative to define themselves. This relational narrative, however, does not present itself as such but instead presents itself as a form of essentialised, yet unrealised, self. At an extreme this can be described as a process of the *governance of an employee's soul* (Willmott 1993) or the corporate *colonisation of the self* (Casey 1995) that purports to create a harmonious accommodation by employees of the preferred selves proffered by the organisation. This colonisation thus acts to 'eliminate or contain undesirable features to achieve appropriate fit between employee and culture . . . [and the] . . . internalization of the values and practices of the new culture' (Casey 1995: 142–3). Here 'employees are enjoined to develop self-images and work orientations that are deemed congruent with managerially defined objectives' (Alvesson and Willmott 2002: 619) such that 'in the name of expanded practical autonomy, [corporate culture] aspires to extend management control by colonizing the affective domain' (Willmott 1993: 517).

An important feature of both Landmark and McKinsey's education is the assumption that the interests of the corporation and the interests of the employees are unproblematically congruent. For Landmark, this means enabling people to access their 'transcendental consciousness' to give them the power that will lead companies to competitive advantage. For McKinsey it means 'liberating' people so that they will contribute to the cultural capital and performance of the organisation. In both cases, the pedagogical approach and content appear to sidestep the possibilities of 'conflicts of interest within organizations that revolve around social divisions of ownership and control' (Willmott 1993: 524) and, furthermore, attempt to talk such potential out of existence by appealing to the 'humanity' of the worker – a humanity that is seen to be manifested in an inevitable formation of identity. Consequently, the discourse of culturalism implies definitionally that to be a true self or to have a fully realised humanity is only achievable when one's interests are aligned with those of the organisation. This in turn provides a discursive justification for the management of culture that attempts to 'redefine the nature of employee identification so as to privilege the organization over other identities' (Parker 2000: 23). Such organisational interests, of course, are unquestioningly capitalist in their orientation – thus an employee can gain personal fulfilment through bringing out their 'true' self and employing that self for the achievement of corporate growth, profitability etc. Although this relationship is not in any way brought into question or problematised in the programme, it is worth noting that the basis for the relationship is an unchanged corporatist agenda. Employees are thus urged to adapt their selves to the achievement of corporate goals. The pedagogical practices employed are designed to produce this change. As described earlier, these pedagogies use structured forms of self-reflection mediated through particular humanistic notions of identity and its relationship to the corporation. Within these pedagogies, the notions of self portrayed by Landmark and McKinsey seem to be developed in an evangelical tenor that proposes their programmes will benefit individuals in an existential manner over and above what they would be able to do without the benefit of these pedagogies. In so doing, McKinsey draws directly on a discourse of 'spirituality', 'self-actualisation' and 'allowing people to be themselves'; similarly, Landmark explicitly refers to a philosophically 'justified' notion of new ways of being. This attainment of the humanist self – autonomous, ethereal and self-actualised – is imbued with a moral virtue. This morality suggests that employees have an essential ethical responsibility to act as agents for the achievement of corporate goals.

The development of concepts and practices associated with corporate culture can also be seen within a historical perspective where post-industrialised workplaces are said to rely less and less on people's physical labour and more on their cognitive and interpretive capacities (Rhodes and Garrick 2000) – a form of 'immaterial labour' (Hardt and Negri 2001) that moves from the management of the outside to the management of the inside of the worker. Here, 'the "autonomous" subjectivity of the productive individual has become a central economic resource' (Miller and Rose 1990: 26.) Such a scenario leads McKinsey's Michael Rennie to predict that 'you're inevitably going to see more programs like this in the near future . . . CEOs are wondering: "How do I get my intangible assets in order?" ' (Rennie cited in Voigt 2002). Indeed, it is this ordering of 'intangible assets' that McKinsey and Landmark's pedagogical practices suggest they can do. Rennie's reference to employees as 'assets' is also noteworthy as it reflects a more general tendency in organisations to metaphorically define people in economic terms – human resources, knowledge assets, intellectual capital and so forth – such that the very nature of being human is conflated with commercial interests (Rhodes and Garrick 2002). The relational identity narrative that both Landmark and McKinsey infer is one where the discourses of the social prevent people from realising their 'true' self; with their assistance people can get back in touch with that self. The implication is that the ongoing process of identity formation and modification in some way ends as one sheds the pretensions and distortions through which one has come to define oneself and realises an ultimate individual and hidden potential – indeed, a potential that can be brought to bear on securing 'success' for the organisation one works for. It seems that it is therefore fortuitous and convenient that helping people realise their true selves is unproblematically aligned with a traditional and unchanged set of corporate goals.

What these programmes imply is a notion of the employee as an 'identity worker who is enjoined to incorporate the new managerial discourses into narratives of self-identity' (Alvesson and Willmott 2002: 622). Arguing, as we have done here, that corporate culture change programmes entail the active attempt to create employee identity in a form that is conducive to a fixed corporatist agenda inevitably begs the question of how effective such an approach can be. To this end, it must be recognised that the identity that a corporation might try to instil among its employees is, of course, only one of the many identities that they must contend with – the process of reflexive identification, although political, is done within a multiplicity of potential self-narratives to which one can relate. Identity, in this sense, is not singular but rather it is an arena of contradiction and conflict where the 'colluded corporate self is an inherently contradictory and unstable identity based on simulated myths of community, consensus, family and solidarity' (Reed 1998: 201). The result can thus only ever be a form of ambivalence that manifests itself in an incomplete internalisation of the organisationally espoused values and behaviours (Casey 1999). As such, the harmonious promises of the pedagogies of corporate culture are recast as power struggles over the very identity of the employee – struggles over who gets to tell the story in which an individual identity is manufactured. Thus the fantasy of control that the corporate culture pedagogies promise will inevitably fail in that the 'organizational regulation of identity . . . is a precarious and often contested process involving active identity work . . . organizational members are not reducible to passive consumers of managerially designed and designated identities' (Alvesson and Willmott 2002: 621).

Our point is that employees are not passive cultural dupes eagerly awaiting an organisational imprimatur to define themselves in particular ways. Employees might react in ways quite different to the promises of the pedagogy; commonly such responses could be expected to include cynicism or resistance. For example, one reaction from employees who participated in a McKinsey programme at Woodside Electricity was the belief that the 'psychological probing' that was involved constituted an invasion of privacy. A senior Woodside official commented: 'This is the closest thing to a corporate cult that I have ever seen. It is extremely damaging to some people. They cannot handle the attempt to so fully integrate the workplace with their private lives' (cited in Treadgold 2002). Indeed, some Woodside staff at all levels chose to resign from the company in response to the new 'love based' approach to management (Treadgold 2002). Thus corporate culture programmes can be expected to result in unplanned consequences; these include resistance to prescribed values and beliefs, subversion of implementation processes and a mimicry of the espoused culture rather than an internalisation of it (Harris and Ogbona 2002).

What this suggests is that the project of cultural pedagogy is never complete and that 'organizational culture is a continually contested process of making claims of difference within and between groups of people who are formally constituted as members of a defined group' (Parker 2000: 233). In the face of organisational change, people at work might reconstruct their identities from the discursive resources available to them, however, the alignment of selves to a newly defined work culture is such that it does not necessarily mean a passive identification with the dictates of given programmes; instead change programmes can result in a struggle over different ways of being that might be more disordered than aligned (Chappell *et al.* 2000). This suggests that the practices of corporate culture that have been discussed here appear to be oversocialised in their claims in that they overemphasise both management capability and worker receptivity to cultural change. They assume that people are eager to accept a managerially defined message in its entirety without reference to other sources of information or perspectives (Collins 1995). Further, in an ironic turn, they focus on identity as the main factor that influences such change: on the one hand individual identity seems to be recognised, yet on the other it is subsumed into the assumed omnipotence of managerial definitions of what such an identity ought to be.

Identity and power struggle

In opening this chapter we suggested that the notion of corporate culture relates to a set of relatively new organisational practices. Noteworthy, however, is that although such practices are new in this context, they are anteceded by a long history of social practices referred to by Foucault (1986) as 'the cultivation of the self'. As Foucault explains, the idea that one has to attend to oneself and care for oneself dates back to ancient Greece; he argues that these ancient notions of caring for oneself were designed to

> enable one to commune with oneself, to recollect one's bygone days, to place the whole of one's life before one's own eyes, to get to know oneself . . . and, by contemplating a life reduced

to its essential, to rediscover the basic principles of rational conduct.

(1986: 50)

An important insight by Foucault is that such care for the self is not an exercise in solitude, but that it is a social practice that took place within institutionalised structures – it is an 'intensification of social relations' (1986: 53) where to care for oneself is related to being cared for by others whose task it is to tutor. Of interest in terms of our example here is how the ancient practices described by Foucault bear a strong resemblance to the current practice of organisational culture, and, more pointedly, how organisations and their hired consultants have taken it upon themselves to assume the role of the ancient tutor and 'wise man'. Organisations perceive themselves to be places where 'the art of self-knowledge [is] developed, with precise recipes, specific forms of examination, and codified exercise' (1986: 58). It is here that individuals are 'summoned into place' within discursive structures and practices (Hall 1996) – indeed, organisational and managerial discourses appear to be increasingly doing this summoning and, further, pedagogy is one of the technologies that is brought to bear in order to do so.

As we have argued, using examples from Landmark and McKinsey, such pedagogy is problematic at three levels. First, it makes the uncritical assumption that personal identity, in its 'true' form, is unproblematically congruent with the interests of business organisations. Second, the existence of such pedagogy assumes that organisations have the right to govern the identity of their employees in order to bring them in line with such a notion of the self. Third, this suggests an arrogant over-socialised perspective of organisations that does not account for the potentially unresolvable power struggles that emerge from attempts to modify the collective and individual identities of employees. A pedagogy of corporate culture is thus part of a more general discourse of corporate culture that has 'tended to read the diversity of practices within organizations through a managerialist lens and consequently underplayed the role of process, meaning and division' (Parker 2000: 26). Indeed, the pedagogical practices reviewed here form an extreme case of this tendency – one that attempts to write particular identities onto people at work and, by claiming those identities to be in some way natural, sidesteps issues of power in the discursive formation of worker identity. It is this power, however, that is a critical component of the way people learn to 'be' at work.

Concluding comments

In concluding this chapter, we now discuss the implications of such power and what they might suggest for identity in organisations. The narratives of identity proposed in the pedagogical practice that we have discussed make the claim that pre-identified and singular definitions of the self have the potential to enact a powerful monologue over people at work. Such a singular view of identity is thus posited as being true, in an eternal and unquestionable sense, such that employees must engage with it or else be positioned as being somehow not fully actualised as persons. In providing a critique of such a claim, however, we have argued that the assertion of such monologic possibilities can only ever be incomplete. In opposition to such a view, we suggest that knowledge and identity are better understood as contested, active, creative and social rather than being pre-existing and fixed. Here, 'reality' is being created in the dialogic intersection of different ways of seeing and talking about the world (Rhodes 2000, 2001, 2002) such that identity is 'the result of a dialogue between different discourses of the self but where some discourses work to establish a loud monologue that drowns out other possibilities' (Rhodes and Garrick 2002: 96).

The pedagogies of corporate culture are an example of such a monologue which, although 'louder, more articulate or more powerful than others' (Hazen 1993: 16), can never be the only story that can be told. The implication is that the 'self' is not a self-sufficient concept, but rather is a relational process that is continuous and provisional (Waugh 1992) where such relations include, but are not limited to, organisationally sanctioned discourses. In terms of pedagogies of organisational identity, the implication is that the forms of identity that such programmes offer are not the 'end game' of identity, but rather a potentially powerful discourse that people at work must deal with. This authoritative discourse of the acculturated work self, however, does not present itself as a participant in a dialogue of the self, but rather claims a position as a monologue. This monologic character of the pedagogy is such that it claims to speak for all – it is a unitary perception of identity. Thus it operates as an authoritative discourse that 'permits no play with the context framing it, no play with its borders, no gradual and flexible transitions . . . it enters the consciousness as a compact and indivisible mass' (Bakhtin 1981: 343). Of course such claims to monologisation, while powerful, are by no means fully realisable – a unitary perspective is something posited rather than given. What this suggests is that particular narratives of identity, such as those embedded in the pedagogies described, can always be relativised against alternatives. This is not to say that the notions of identity put forward by corporate culture are equal to others, but rather that they operate in relation to, and possibly in conflict with, the other self-perceptions that people bring to work. The result is a dialogic struggle over identity. It is here that the discourse of the self presented by culturalism can be seen as being problematic because it fails to acknowledge such struggle. Thus for organisations 'autonomy is represented as a gift that can be bestowed by culture upon employees rather than something that individuals struggle to realize' (Willmott 1993: 527).

Of course, suggesting that people's identity in organisations is predictable and manageable is seductive. Dialogue and democracy are not so easy and culturalism offers a pain-free alternative which 'enables each employee to conform to a modern (humanist) sense of self, as a self-determining individual, without the burden of responsibility – the angst – that accompanies the making of (existential) choices between ultimate conflicting values' (Willmott 1993: 527). Nevertheless, in practice identity is not 'easy' – it is something that must be worked at. Further, the pre-eminence of work as an important part of people's lives implies that work and identity cannot be easily separated; people's identity will always be dialogically intertwined with the nature and demands of their work. In providing a critique of the pedagogies described in this chapter, it is not enough to claim them to be problematic, as if to suggest that organisations should somehow cease to influence the identities of their employees. Such influence is inevitable – it is not a question of whether organisations influence identity, but more a question of how they influence identity. If nothing else, the discourse of corporate culture and its attendant pedagogies reflect a realisation on the part of business organisations that such a process exists and that people do actually possess an identity, a humanity. The issue to be raised, however, is to what extent has this realisation gone far enough – in particular, to what extent has it enabled the organisation of work to explore territories outside of an instrumental teleology that sees financial success as the *only* possible measure of success, and identity manipulation as a means for achieving it. What this calls for is pedagogical practices that allow a 'search for new modes of existence and government practices based on dialogue and reflexivity . . . [implying] . . . the acceptance of plurality and diversity that constitute society and the recognition of diverse lifestyle with their dilemmas and paradoxes' (Ibarra-Colado 2002: 180).

Chapter 7

Games as a pedagogy in HIV/AIDS education

Protecting oneself

> Young people occupy the border zones between the mythic poles
> of adult-child, sexual and asexual, rational-emotional, civilised-
> savage, and productive-unproductive.
>
> (Lesko 1996: 455)

Introduction

Despite recent advances in treatment, acquired immune deficiency
syndrome (AIDS) remains a major global health concern. While efforts
have been made to find effective cures, current treatments remain
costly and out of reach of the majority of people who are human
immunodeficiency virus (HIV) positive. During the 1980s, when no
effective treatments were available, many health experts and policymakers took the view that HIV/AIDS-related health education, particularly for 'at risk' groups, was probably the most effective way
of minimising the spread of the infection. Indeed, there remains a
broad consensus that the modification of high-risk behaviours such
as unprotected sexual activities or the sharing of needles in intrave-
nous drug use remains the single most effective way of reducing HIV
infection rates.

A large number of HIV/AIDS education programmes have been
introduced worldwide, specifically designed to achieve behavioural
change in specific social and cultural groups regarded as being particularly 'at risk'. In this context young people are constructed as one
such 'at risk' group.[1] HIV/AIDS research concerning young people
also points to 'homelessness' as a key risk factor in infection (Johnson
et al. 1996). Researchers in this area have commonly utilised the
individual-society dualism outlined in Chapter 1 when constructing
their story of 'homeless young people'. For example, Crawford et al.
(1997) and Johnson et al. (1996) take an individual and psychological

position, highlighting 'risk' in terms of cognitive and behavioural 'deficiencies' that are used to explain unsafe sexual practices among homeless young people. From this point of view, young people are seen as having illusions of immortality and invulnerability. They fail to grasp the long-term consequences of their current set of behaviours. They have insufficient cognitive and behavioural skills to implement risk reduction strategies such as negotiating the use of condoms and have inappropriate beliefs and myths concerning sexuality, HIV and AIDS. On the other hand, researchers such as Greenblatt and Robinson (1993) take a more sociological perspective, noting that the 'high risk' behaviours of homeless young people are usually driven by immediate survival needs and the strategies they deploy are essentially those required to maintain their own precarious existence. Moreover, their homelessness is often the result of being part of a family/ community 'at risk'.

Either way, the use of the individual-society dualism by researchers to provide normative explanations regarding 'homeless young people' does important work in fostering particular pedagogical interventions designed to reduce 'high risk' behaviours. In this chapter we focus on the evolution of one Australian HIV/AIDS education programme known as the 'HOT game', originally designed for 'homeless' young people, a group regarded as being particularly 'at risk' in HIV/AIDS literature. We do this not to make some judgement about the quality or effectiveness of the programme or the competence of the youth workers who design and implement it. Rather, through our investigation we seek to interrogate what implicit theorisations of the self are embedded in the programme. What learning activities are deployed and to what effect? What kinds of stories are being told regarding young people and what identities are being constructed? In short, we wish to focus on the contingent relationships that exist between pedagogy, identity and narrative.

In order to answer these questions we examine the written materials associated with the programme, including the facilitator's guide, and the pedagogical practices that are utilised. Our other source of information comes from conversations with the coordinator who was part of the team that developed the programme and a team member who facilitates workshops for youth workers involved with 'homeless' young people.

Making the game

The HOT game was devised by a health outreach team employed by an urban, government-funded youth accommodation agency involved in the operation and management of refuges and medium- and long-term accommodation services for homeless young people. Originally this small group of project workers was employed to design and deliver health promotion resources for homeless young people involved with the agency.

In 1991, the agency started a project that specifically addressed the issue of HIV/AIDS and young people. Mike (pseudonym), the current coordinator, began working on the project from a resource development perspective. The intention was to design useful resources that would on the one hand provide essential information about HIV/AIDS in terms of the disease, its transmission and prevention while at the same time providing this information in ways that would engage young people with the issues involved. The aim of this intervention was to change the high-risk behaviours of young people.

As Mike put it, the premise at the time was that in order to get the message across the information resources needed to be 'fun and colourful for the kids'. Using focus groups of young people and youth workers to assist in the design of resources that might work, a great deal of effort was put into designing posters and information booklets that provided young people with general knowledge about HIV/AIDS. The use of these focus groups was originally seen as the best way to ensure that the resources would be understood and appreciated by the target audience. Sets of materials were developed and distributed over the next two years to youth refuges, drop-in centres and group homes.

A local museum was at the time developing an exhibition that focused on important contemporary issues and wanted to include an exhibit about young people and HIV/AIDS. So the group used this opportunity to develop the first interactive prototype of the game – a museum exhibit. The prototype was designed as a walk-through exhibition where people could participate in interactive activities created to inform them about issues concerning young people and HIV/AIDS.

As a result of this experience the team considered that HIV/AIDS education was an area that required facilitation. Information about HIV/AIDS related issues, even if packaged to engage young people, was insufficient and unlikely to change the behaviour of the target group. Consequently they moved away from the idea of providing stand-alone information and began to look at ways of developing resources in which delivery could be facilitated.

The team noticed that during focus groups with young people and youth workers they seemed as much in the business of facilitating conversations about sexual matters between young people and youth workers as they were getting ideas about what kinds of resources about HIV/AIDS would work with young people. This observation, together with the museum experience, led to a major change in direction in terms of the work of the team. Rather than seeing themselves as simply resource developers, they now considered themselves as providing resources and strategies that would initiate conversations between young people and youth workers about issues of sex, sexuality and health.

As Mike put it, the team realised that many youth workers were not confident or comfortable delivering explicit information to young people about sex, sexuality, sexual health and injecting drug use. The issues involved were very confronting for both young people and youth workers. Yet these issues were essential elements in any HIV/AIDS education programme. Moreover, youth workers working in accommodation services and drop-in centres were ideally placed to provide ongoing health education and information to homeless young people who were considered most at risk.

The team therefore began to develop a 'game' that could be played by young people, which provided a 'safe' vehicle through which youth workers and young people could have conversations about sex and sexual health, the game acting as a device to begin such conversations. The HOT game evolved as a board game similar to Trivial Pursuit. It incorporates questions, answers and activities. Individuals and teams can play it. It can be adapted to be competitive with teams competing with each other for 'points' to win. The game uses many interactive teaching-learning strategies and since its inception it has, with support from the team, been adapted by different youth workers to accommodate young people of different ages, genders, literacy levels, cultural backgrounds, interests and locations.

Today the work of the team not only involves facilitating the game with homeless young people but also providing training workshops for youth workers where they experience the game and begin the process of adapting it for their particular youth groups. Up to 500 young people and youth workers have been involved in one way or another with the game's development and today over 50 different versions have been produced. Moreover, regular evaluations conducted by the team indicate that youth workers find the game extremely useful in their practice.

Playing the game

To play the game the board is set up with a number of game categories. Players take turns to answer questions and participate in activities related to HIV/AIDS, sexually transmitted infections (STIs), hepatitis C, safe sex and safe drug use. The game categories include:

- **All play.** A set of questions or activities that any player can answer or do.
- **Drug stuff.** A set of questions about alcohol and drug use.
- **How safe? hep C.** Players must decide how safe certain activities are in terms of hepatitis C infection and categorise them as SAFE, SAFE IF . . . or NOT SAFE.
- **How safe? HIV.** Players must decide how safe certain activities are in terms of HIV infection and categorise them as SAFE, SAFE IF . . . or NOT SAFE.
- **Sticky stuff.** A set of multiple choice questions about various sexually transmitted diseases.
- **Tell 'em where to go.** A range of scenarios are described and players are asked to offer suggestions as to where people can go for help, support or advice in relation to each scenario.
- **What am I?** A player is given the name of a sexually transmitted disease and other players have to guess what is it by asking questions. Only YES or NO answers are allowed.
- **The heat is on.** A particular scenario where pressure from one person is being applied to another regarding such things as safe sex and drug use. Players are asked to discuss what the person should do in this scenario (there are no right or wrong answers in this activity).
- **Xena and Hercules.** The card poses a problem in relation to sex, safe sex and sexuality in an 'agony aunt' format and players are encouraged to offer advice.
- **Party zone.** Each card has a party scenario and players must brainstorm ideas about reducing harm associated with drugs and alcohol in a party environment.
- **What's that?** The cards ask questions about contraception and safe sex.

- **Action station.** This is an all activity category with teams and players asked to do activities such as a 'condom race'.
- **Question box.** This is a category where the player must write down a question that they want answered at the end of the HOT game.

As the game board is divided into only seven areas the facilitator of the game can select from the categories above, enabling the game to be targeted to particular issues that the group of young people believe are of most importance to them. The facilitator can also sort the cards allowing for certain questions and topics to come at the top of the card stack.

The game begins with an individual or team spinning a bottle or arrow, which determines the first category to be answered. Each category has a series of game cards, which either ask a specific question or require the players to undertake a particular activity. Points can be allocated according to the question or activity that is asked of the players. Each individual or team takes their turn by spinning the bottle on the game board. The game lasts for about an hour or more.

In many ways the game categories utilise many of the teaching and training strategies and activities commonly used in adult education (see Chapter 1). Most of the activities draw on the individual and collective experiences and reflections of the players. Indeed, their purpose often reflects those outlined by Taylor *et al.* (2000) cited in Chapter 1. For example, some of the game activities help young people to 'define, own, name and claim their own experience'. Others assist young people to 'discern and name the underlying patterns, structures and limiting beliefs that block a group's vision'. Still others, such as 'The heat is on' 'introduce a strategy to stand above or outside both their rational and intuitive selves'. Indeed, overall, the HOT game is an example of those types of educational strategies that seek to change attitudes, beliefs, understanding and behaviours' (see Taylor *et al.* 2000).

However, the game does not privilege particular ways of being in the world or particular youthful identities. Indeed, most game players can find something of themselves in the game. For example, it recognises (and therefore allows) diverse identities and different youthful behaviours to coexist. As a young person playing the game one can be chaste, promiscuous or anything in between. The game recognises different sexual identities. A young person can be straight, gay or bisexual. The game also acknowledges different kinds of youthful subject positions based on gender, social and cultural norms. It refuses judgement on any of these identities. What it does do is provide information about safe sex and examines different behaviours that reduce the possibility of infection for people with particular identities.

In short, the identity work the game does is not to construct or privilege particular youthful identities but to recognise the variety of subject positions held by youth. Moreover, this particular take on variation is understood and acted on through the recognition of individual difference rather than through invocation of large sociological categories to explain identity formation (this contrasts with the gender-oriented programmes discussed in the next chapter).

The youth worker as facilitator receives a guide which provides extensive support materials that include straightforward descriptions of sexually transmitted infections (STIs) and explicit information that can be drawn on to answer the game questions and produce the scenarios. Youth workers are also encouraged to experience the game prior to using it by participating in a workshop where they play the game and then reflect on its use with the young people that they work with.

Theory and the game

The original purpose of the HOT game was to act as a catalyst for changing the behaviour of homeless young people to reduce the risk of infection from HIV/AIDS and other sexually transmitted diseases. However, as the game developed it also became a catalyst for changing the way youth workers engaged young people in health education activities. This was by no means an outcome predicted by the team who conceptualised, designed and developed the original resources. Nevertheless, it has now become a defining feature of the game in the context of health education for homeless young people involved with the agency and is now regarded by the development team as a crucial component of their work.

In order to explore this change programme in more detail we now turn to the context in which the development team undertook their work. We want to uncover what theoretical perspectives grounded the work of the project team in order to make sense of their pedagogical interventions in the lives of young people and youth workers.

Although the project team is employed by a youth accommodation agency a government health department funds the team's work. The team is accountable to the management of the youth accommodation agency and works within certain agency guidelines. The coordinator believes that this structure has given the team 'an exceptional amount of freedom' in terms of developing appropriate materials, a degree of freedom that he suggests would be unthinkable in a government department. This freedom was also an outcome of the health 'crisis' that emerged with the onset of HIV/AIDS infections in Australia in the late 1980s.

According to Mike, the team conceptualised, developed and implemented the HOT game 'organically'. That is, they did not define their practice with reference to particular theories. Rather, they 'followed their noses', experimented, used anecdotal market research and intuition, and learned from their mistakes.

However, it would be a mistake to suggest that the work of this group was without theory. Indeed, one of the more remarkable features of our investigation has been the extent to which explicit reference is made, by the development team, to a number of theoretical positions in the areas of health, education and change. For example, the team works within a 'harm minimisation framework' with regard to sexual health and drug use among young people. The position taken by the team is that the principle of harm minimisation is one of responding to the reality of a situation, and minimising the damage that may be caused to an individual or a community as a result of that situation. The team's position is predicated on the view that abstinence or 'zero tolerance' are not realistic options for many young people. In short, the team based the game on providing a number of options that young people could use to either reduce or eliminate the possibility of infection from HIV or other blood-borne diseases. For the team, abstinence was one option among others.

Conversations with Mike also reveal that he regards the development team, and indeed most youth workers, as operating from a cultural action paradigm. According to Mike, phrases such as 'empowerment', 'taking control', 'participation', 'community development' and 'giving youth a voice' are commonly used in conversations about the purpose and direction of the team's work and youth work more generally. In many ways this position is consistent with a long-standing sociological theorisation of young people, most clearly articulated by work undertaken within the Centre for Contemporary Cultural Studies (CCCS) in Birmingham, England, beginning in the late 1970s. The theoretical assumption underpinning much of this work uses a social control model to explain young people as a sociological category and explore the relationship between youth, power and culture.

At the risk of oversimplification, this model explains the behaviour of young people as emanating from their reaction and resistance to their experience of dominating forms of social control. These control mechanisms are in turn commonly associated within neo-Marxist accounts of social power, with youth struggling to liberate itself from various forms of oppressive social control. From this perspective, youth work is about providing young people with the resources to recognise and 'do something about' their social oppression. Freirian cultural action in many ways has been used by the team to frame their intervention. As Mike said:

> [Cultural action] was the buzz-word with everyone in the team. I guess everything we did related to that. The way we sequenced everything. We started off with very physical things, then with naming the world, then doing something with the information like making a product, then instigating some action.

Thus in many ways the development team draws on what we refer to in Chapter 1 as a *critical pedagogy* or *social action tradition*. And as was outlined in Chapter 1 this position tends to use a conception of self that is socially constituted with the attendant danger of the self becoming 'over socialised' or 'over determined', unable to recognise, without help, the oppressive social forces that limit the emergence of a 'true self'.

The team also drew explicitly on other theories including action research (Kemmis and McTaggart 1988), experiential learning and adult learning in the continuous development and redevelopment of the game. As Mike put it, the game was designed so that it could continually change and adapt to new priorities, cultural norms and local circumstances.

However, the team also used other theoretical positions to inform their work in terms of behavioural change. For example, a position paper produced for the team reviewed a number of HIV/AIDS and related health education programmes directed at young people. The paper identifies a number of behavioural change and social learning theories that have underpinned such programmes.

Aspects of social learning theory are incorporated in some programmes (Kirby *et al.* 1997). Exposed to various scenarios, learners learn to recognise social influences and to practise assertive communication and resistance skills. Other programmes have adopted the Health Belief Model (Jantz and Becker 1984) which provides

explanations as to why some people do not take precautionary measures to prevent illnesses. Using this model, programmes have been
designed to increase at risk groups perceived susceptibility to HIV/
AIDS infection. Still more programmes have been based on Social
Inoculation Theory (Geiger and Tierney 1996). In these programmes,
participants' attitudes, beliefs and decisions are rehearsed and tested
in simulated situations in order to inform and strengthen 'healthy'
decision making by participants in the programme.

The work of Dryfoos (1991) and Rogers (1984) has also been used
in HIV/AIDS programmes. These ideas suggest that participants are
likely to change high-risk behaviours if they are able to estimate their
own risk of acquiring HIV/AIDS and believe themselves capable of
adapting their behaviour to reduce the threat of infection.

Overall these theoretical positions, in different ways, reveal the
ongoing tensions concerning conceptions of the self that are either
based on a construction which privileges an essential individuality or
one in which the self emerges as a product of the social world – the
individual-society dualism.

In the facilitation guide, the development team makes both explicit
and implicit reference to many of these theoretical positions stating
that the game has been developed using a synthesis of various concepts,
approaches and theories: 'We hope to provide an alternative to the
"banking" system of education where we the "expert educators"
deposit the message (safe sex/IDU [Intravenous Drug Use]) into the
learners' "empty" heads'.

All change

Although the team originally set out with the goal of changing the
'high risk' behaviour of young people, as the quote above demonstrates
they also (albeit more implicitly) set out to change the behaviour of
youth workers at the same time. The HOT game became in effect a
pedagogical strategy used to change both youth workers and young
people, albeit in different ways as shown on p. 119.

All change strategies involve participants either doing things 'differently' and/or doing things 'better'. Either way, a change strategy is
largely predicated on a number of assumptions that are used to construct participants prior to the implementation of the change strategy. How these constructions are discursively developed within the
context of the HOT game provides us with useful insights concerning
the ways in which the identities of both youth workers and homeless

Youth workers and change
Essentially the team wanted to raise the priority of sexual health education in the everyday work of youth accommodation agency workers. These workers were in an ideal position to engage with young people about matters of sexual health, however they did not give this a high priority in their work. The team identified a number of barriers that prevented sexual health education being given a high priority. These included:

- lack of knowledge on sexual health issues among workers
- lack of resources and time to develop and implement programmes
- lack of confidence talking about sexual and drug-related matters with young people.

The game was designed to address these issues and increase the priority given to health issues by youth workers.

Young people and change
The team wanted to change certain behaviours of young people in order to reduce the incidence of HIV/AIDS and other blood-borne viruses and STIs. The specific youth targets were homeless young people. Many research findings suggested that young people's behaviour meant that they were more likely to be exposed to these infections, while other research indicated that homeless young people were at an even greater risk of contracting HIV/AIDS and other sexually transmitted diseases than their peers. Homeless young people often:

- lack information regarding sexual health and safe sex practices
- lack the cognitive and behavioural skills required to reduce high-risk behaviours
- were driven into high-risk behaviours by immediate and pressing survival needs.

young people are constructed. The facilitator's guide was the main pedagogical device designed to produce the changes in the way youth workers undertook their work, while the HOT game was the pedagogical device designed to change the behaviours of homeless young people involved with the accommodation agency. We now look at the ways in which both young people and youth workers are constructed by analysing these pedagogical devices.

Constructing youth workers

The facilitator's guide addresses all of the identified barriers that the team saw as preventing youth workers giving sexual health a high priority in their work with homeless young people. The guide provides detailed but non-technical information about sexually transmitted diseases, symptoms, causes etc. Consequently it provides youth workers with the knowledge of sexual health that they might lack. It also provides the resources, support materials and detailed instructions that are needed to facilitate the HOT game with young people.

Perhaps more importantly, the game format provides youth workers with a vehicle through which they can talk 'safely' and confidently with young people about extremely personal, sensitive (and on occasion difficult legal) issues. The game gives the workers and young people space in which to talk about issues that are raised by the game rather than by either youth workers or young people as such. In some senses the game acts as the 'absent authority', leaving young people and youth workers to more freely discuss what this 'authority' is telling them.

However, the facilitator's guide does more than this. It can also be viewed as a narrative that constructs a particular professional identity for youth workers involved in accommodation services. Youth workers encourage 'self-determination and critical thinking' among young people. Their work with young people is grounded 'in the reality of young peoples' social and economic relations'. According to the guide youth workers 'encourage young people, collectively and individually, to take action to tackle the barriers to safe sex and drug use practices'. In short, the guide deploys the discourses of cultural action to construct a particular professional identity for youth workers.

The guide also signals itself as a change pedagogy for youth workers. It constructs youth workers as facilitators of learning by drawing on the discourses of various pedagogical traditions of adult education. In particular it uses the widely endorsed 'learning from experience' as a central pedagogical technology. It foregrounds the need for youth workers who facilitate the HOT game not only to recognise and act on issues of difference but to draw on different experiences as a resource for learning. For example, youth workers are called on to recognise differences:

- **In knowledge:** 'Young people bring to the group a considerable amount of experience and knowledge. The facilitator may be more of an expert in terms of sexual health and HIV/AIDS information, but the game participants are the experts on themselves.'
- **In contexts:** 'Ideas of safer sex need to be discussed within the context of people's lives and experiences. Personal and social

factors which may represent a barrier to safe sex for people are often specific to individuals.'

- **In sexuality:** 'You need to be aware that not all group members are heterosexual. Even if you don't know what people's sexuality is, it should not be presumed that they are heterosexual. Safe sex information must include discussion of homosexual and hetero-sexual sex.'

- **In culture:** 'An individual's background and culture will influence the way they perceive information about sexual health. You will need to be aware of these differences.'

The guide also calls for the facilitator to be critically reflexive when facilitating the game. 'you need to be critically aware of your own assumptions regarding cultural, gender and sexual diversity – to be careful of the language you choose, the humour you use and your body language – to embrace difference and not exclusion'.

In many ways therefore this narrative constructs youth workers in ways that are consistent with what the team regard as the dominant theoretical position (cultural action) that underpins the professional practice of youth workers. However, the guide is also a narrative that seeks to change, reinforce or legitimise particular approaches taken by youth workers when working with young people in the area of sexual health education. These include the critical pedagogy/social action tradition, but also pedagogical practices drawn from experiential learning and critical reflection (see Chapter 1), with which youth workers may be less familiar.

In short, in contrast to the game, the facilitator's guide 'makes up' particular professional identities for youth accommodation workers.

Constructing young people

The HOT game is the pedagogical strategy with which the development team aims to change the behaviour of young people to reduce the risk of infection from HIV/AIDS and other blood-borne diseases. As we saw above, in order for the HOT game to achieve this outcome, particular professional identities and particular pedagogical technologies are deployed by the development team in the facilitator's guide. However, the HOT game was also developed using a number of assumptions concerning young people.

First, homeless young people do not want to be told what to do as they have valid experiences which can be acknowledged in the game format. Second, the game format allows serious subjects to be approached in a lighter and less threatening way than other approaches to sexual health education. Third, this format acknowledges that some young people already have considerable knowledge and experience which is recognised using the game format. Finally, this format allows young people to analyse particular actions and experiences and modify or rehearse alternative responses in a safe and simulated environment.

Another important characteristic of the HOT game is its attempt to manage the issue of difference and young people. In some senses its guiding assumption is that homeless young people are not the same. Consequently, the game provides players with a wide variety of scenarios and activities that reflect issues of difference in terms of gender, cultural norms, sexuality and prior knowledge and experience of sex and sexual health issues. This assumption is carried further by the flexibility built into the game that allows particular issues to be foregrounded or provides the youth worker with information regarding how to adapt the game to better meet the needs of particular groups of young people. The issue of difference is also addressed by the collective experience of playing the game with others, which provides a platform on which alternative views can be explored and discussed.

The game format also assumes that providing information regarding sexual health to homeless young people is insufficient if the goal is to change high-risk behaviours. It therefore rejects the idea that homeless young people are at greater risk because they lack sufficient knowledge concerning sexual health. Rather, it suggests that this information only has meaning for young people if it is presented and discussed in terms of their lives and relationships with others.

Finally, this format does not set out to promote single solutions to high-risk behaviours such as 'safe sex'. Rather, it offers a variety of possible choices for young people in terms of modifying their behaviour. For example, the 'How safe? HIV' category identifies a whole range of behaviours that are either SAFE, SAFE IF . . . or NOT SAFE. These behaviours include: toe-sucking; massage; masturbation; snorting drugs; anal sex with condoms and lube; frottaging with clothes on; abstinence; blood transfusion; sex with lots of partners; sex with someone you trust; giving oral sex to a woman; sharing a mixing spoon for drugs; giving oral sex to a man; injecting drugs; being on the pill; using gladwrap instead of condoms; pulling out before cumming; unprotected sex with a long-term partner; fisting; rimming; and using dams for oral sex with a woman. As can be seen from this list the game does not make judgements concerning the possible sexual and social experiences of homeless young people. Rather, it assumes that they are very diverse in terms of their experiences, which are in many ways reflections of other broader personal, social, cultural and sexual orientations and experiences of individual young people. Moreover, in many of the activities emphasis is placed on finding any number of possible responses to particular scenarios that young people may find themselves.

The developers of the game go to great lengths to avoid normalising homeless young people. They emphasise difference throughout the game and utilise it as a pedagogical resource central to the playing of the game. They make no claim to provide definitive answers concerning the 'best' or 'most correct' ways of responding to situations which have a greater chance of leading to infection, but provide players with, or elicit from them possible ways of managing such a situation. The aim of the game is to enable the players to create for themselves a life history or 'reflexive narrative' concerning their own sexual health (see Chapter 3).

However, the normalising of homeless young people cannot be fully avoided. The developers of the game, youth workers and young people themselves all exist within a much broader narrative that constructs homeless young people in particular ways. In short, the game players of HOT (and the facilitators for that matter) are already 'made up' by social and cultural definitions prior to the game. Consequently, they also draw on these narrative resources that are 'outside of themselves', an example of what we refer to in Chapter 3 as 'relational narrative'.

For example, the facilitator's guide begins by stating that the HOT game 'is a health promotion project targeting *homeless* and *(at risk) young people*'. Consequently, this narrative already constructs the identity of the game's target group (albeit with 'at risk' appearing in parenthesis indicating a degree of uncertainty regarding this category). As we have argued elsewhere this narrative is not merely descriptive, representing the reality of the situation of the accommodation agency and the youth workers. Rather, it also does particular kinds of discursive work, 'making up' particular youthful identities.

Homeless, 'at risk', young people are the taken for granted constructions in the professional narrative of youth workers, psychologists, government agencies and youth researchers. They are in effect part of the world-making discourses of professionals working with young people and are important sense-making constructions that provide a focus and rationale for professional youth work. However, at the same time they also construct particular youthful identities, giving them certain characteristics, attributes and dispositions that are used to distinguish this group from 'others'.

Young people

Most professional narratives that speak of youth and young people construct the 'essential' youthful experience as a period in which young people undergo physiological, psychological, cognitive and emotional development. Youth is the time of rebellion. It is the time of hormonal upheaval (Polk 1993). It is the time of increased sexual and social experimentation (Humphries 1991). It is the time of psychological disturbance. It is a time critical to the process of identity formation (Erikson 1977). It is the time when peer pressure is at its greatest. It is the time of changing relationships with parents. It is the time when young people are no longer children but nor are they adults. It is the time of transition from school to work (Misko 1999; OECD 1999). It is the time when young people are no longer fully dependent but are not yet independent (Furlong and Cartmel 1997).

These knowledgeable discourses produce significant consequences in terms of the ways in which the identities of young people are socially constructed, not least of which has been a common tendency for youth 'professionals' to take a 'youth as problem' approach to their work. Youth constructed as problem revolves around the idea that many young people experience various forms of alienation in their journey to adulthood. They often display feelings of estrangement from society in general, from their own peers and from particular social institutions such as family and school. Commonly, the causes of alienation are characterised as falling into two broad categories. The first involves focusing on social structural issues such as unemployment or urban decay. The second suggests that alienation emerges out of particular social psychological factors that cause individuals to feel estranged from their immediate social milieux (Giroux 1998).

Subculture or Resistance Theory (see Tait 2000) has, over the last 20 years or more, dominated explanations concerning the 'problem' of youth and remains a significant sense-making construction for youth workers and researchers. This theory uses narratives of class, ideology, economic and cultural oppression to explain 'problem' youth. Groups of young people establish particular oppositional codes of behaviour, styles and ways of relating to the world. In other words, they establish particular subcultures as ways of countering or resisting deep-seated and pervasive social, cultural and economic modes of oppression. As Tait (2000: 2) puts it, '[a]ll in all, the subcultural youth represents a troubled stage of life, its many problems a measure of society's dysfunctionality'.

The influence of these narratives (perhaps unsurprisingly given that the HOT team is made up of 'youth professionals') can be found in their work. For example, the use of a cultural action paradigm in the development of the game is consistent with a view of youth constructed by Resistance or Subculture Theory. Indeed, as the team point out, they put great effort into drawing on the oppositional codes as represented in youth 'language' and 'style' in the development of the resource materials. They use focus groups and trial materials with young people to ensure as much as possible that what is produced appeals to them.

The adoption of a 'harm minimisation' approach to health education in many ways also revolves around ideas of young people constructed as 'rebellious', 'sexually-active', subject to 'peer pressure' and open to social and sexual 'experimentation'. Moreover, the basis of many of the scenarios produced for the game, such as those in 'The heat is on', presuppose these ideas concerning young people.

Homeless young people

The narrative of 'homelessness' can also be viewed as a purely descriptive term within the context of the work of the HOT team. After all, the team is employed by a youth accommodation agency. Therefore, only young people who are both homeless and involved with the accommodation agency play the HOT game. Further, those youth workers who facilitate the game work on a daily basis with the issue of homelessness. Indeed, one of the difficulties experienced by the HOT team has been to increase the priority given to sexual health education by youth workers who primarily work to find accommodation for young people involved with the agency.

However, the need to provide sexual health education to these young people is not based on their homelessness *per se* but rather on homelessness being a narrative that inscribes a constellation of other factors. Within the context of youth professionals, homelessness signals family stress or breakdown, physical and/or emotional abuse, sexual assault, incest, poverty, schooling difficulties, institutionalisation and mental breakdown. In other words, to be homeless brings with it a whole raft of other problems. Johnson *et al.* (1996), for example, identify young people who are homeless, runaways, or who support themselves through the street economy of drugs, prostitution, pan-handling and crime, as HIV/AIDS high-risk populations. Moreover, these narratives do important work by providing the rationale for the development of programmes such as HOT, which are designed to minimise some of the specific risks such as HIV/AIDS infection that are associated with homelessness.

Indeed, without these narratives youth agencies such as that which employs the HOT team would be less able to act as effective advocates for homeless young people or receive the necessary funding for their work. This is not meant to imply that these narratives are without merit or (worse still) untrue representations, cynically designed to maximise funding. Rather it is meant to point out that 'homelessness' and all that it has come to infer is a narrative that is 'true' only with-in one logic of representation. It does not describe individual young people in their lifeworlds as they may or may not have experienced any or all of the characteristics inscribed by 'homelessness'. Rather, 'homelessness' has become one risk factor in a sea of risk identified by government, youth agencies and youth work professionals.

'At risk' young people

Youth 'at risk' is currently the talk of governments, psychologists, sociologists, youth workers and educators when speaking of young people. This discursive shift from the earlier representation of 'prob-lem' youth to 'at risk' youth is significant as it represents more than simply a shift in semantics. It does different discursive work, producing a substantial change in the story of youth.

Youth does not exist as an existential fact but rather is the product of particular modes of reasoning which make the world thinkable. The same is also true for 'problem' youth. As was outlined above, knowledgeable discourses such as psychology and sociology are deployed, as are the discourses of professional expertise (of youth workers and researchers), to construct 'problem' youth – an example of the ways in which discourses are said to actively 'make up' people (du Gay 1996a: 54).

However, despite obvious differences in the various professional discourses that have actively made up problem youth, their point of departure is similar. The object of study is youth – i.e. individual young people in their lifeworlds. Using various techniques such as case study, observation and interview, the lives of young people are examined and the discourses of sociology, psychology and professional expertise are used to provide explanations of particular youth problems. These explanations strive to make connections between cause and effect and then make claims to greater understanding and suggest possible solutions to the various 'problems' of youth.

The recent deployment of 'at risk' in relation to youth is a significant departure from these previous orientations and is yet another example of the way in which 'risk' is receiving much more attention in recent times (Beck 1992; Giddens 1994). The use of the term 'at risk' in the context of youth is the latest narrative that works to manage or govern the way the story of youth comes to be socially realised. It constructs particular categories of young people as being 'at risk' using a wide range of 'risk' factors that include: low academic ability; unemployment; homelessness; dysfunctional family life; ethnicity; poverty etc. These factors are then variously combined to predict the potential futures for young people and then used to justify particular interventions in young people's lives.

However, the deployment of risk in this context does more than this. As Ewald (1991) writes, risk has meaning only in reference to statistical probabilities based on the logic of large numbers. Risk relates therefore to populations not individuals. 'At risk youth' hence emerges through the deployment of various technologies of government including particular information sources, demographic classifications and statistical techniques. Consequently, unlike previous constructions of 'problem' youth, where individuals and their lifeworlds remain the object of analysis, the contemporary notion of at risk youth displaces the notion of the individual with various statistically derived facts and figures that have meaning only in relation to populations. Therefore, the object of analysis and action becomes the multiple sets of risk factors collected by government agencies that are not only used to identify youth at risk but also to articulate and justify the need for specific interventions (Castel 1991).

Thus the players involved in the HOT game are in many ways already 'made up' through professional narratives of youth, homelessness and risk. Moreover, while these narratives are rarely mentioned by those involved in the HOT game they nevertheless do important work in terms of constructing the identity of the HOT game players.

Concluding comments

Educational narratives commonly construct the learner as the recipient of other people's knowledge, albeit mediated by the intervention of the teacher. Indeed, in many ways these narratives require a teaching identity in order to constitute a learning identity. However, the HOT story provides a more complex and contingent account of learner identity. Here, teaching and learning identities are taken up and put down at various points in the development and implementation of the game. Subject positions in the game are not fixed but relational, highly dependent on the context and moment. The youth worker, for example, is a facilitator at one moment and a learner the next. The young person is provided with knowledge of HIV/AIDS on some occasions and called on to provide knowledge on others. The developers of the game provide information regarding HIV/AIDS infection, yet learn from young people how this information can be made more meaningful to them. In some senses the HOT game disrupts the pedagogical identities of teachers and learners constructed by traditional educational narratives. This does not mean that these identities do not exist in the HOT game but rather that they are more fluid and open to transposition. In short, who is the teacher and who is the learner in the HOT game is not straightforward.

In many ways the pedagogical strategies deployed in the HOT game are unremarkable. As we observed elsewhere, versions of learning through reflection on experience are widely endorsed by educators, particularly those involved in fostering certain kinds of self-change and transformation. We have also argued earlier that the use of this pedagogical approach generally involves strategies designed to explore different ways of viewing the world and the production of new models that guide future action.

The development team are also quite explicit about their pedagogical approach, basing it on Freirian critical pedagogy and social action. Here the aim is to produce some collective identification and the sharing of experiences and tacit knowledge with the goal of producing a transformed self through a change in the assumptions and perceptions that the individual uses to interpret the world. The explicit use of difference in the HOT game provides the challenge to individuals' pre-existing assumptions and perceptions. However, the game avoids providing single answers but goes to great lengths to provide a variety of alternatives, leaving open the possibility for the young game players to recognise something of themselves in the game and be

better able in the future to respond to 'the shifting tides of circumstance' (Gergen and Kaye 1992: 255).

Note

1 A definition of 'young people' is not straightforward. Different governments
use different age ranges. The World Association of Research Professionals
defines a young person as between 14–17. The youth accommodation
agency referred to in this chapter works with young people in this age
range.

Chapter 8

Social movements and programmes of gender change

Interrupting oneself

Introduction

This chapter takes as its case study a type of new programme that was initiated across many sectors of education and in many different countries in the latter part of the twentieth century (see Kelly 1989; Coats 1996). This many-pronged initiative takes as its interest issues of gender and as its formal concern some interest in producing changes in the gendered subject who is the student of the programme, and the gendered patterns of social outcomes which are produced from education.

The imperative for these new types of programmes came from a social movement (the Women's Movement), from government policies and interests in extending women's participation in the workforce, sometimes from new legal requirements, often from individual teachers, sometimes from books and theorists. The actual programmes and pedagogies take a number of forms, and the purpose of this chapter is to discuss some different 'technologies' of pedagogy that were associated with this movement, as well as some different conceptions of learners and identity that different programmes represent. The technologies and conceptions of learner subjects discussed here are not unique to this particular area of adult education, but the movement or set of initiatives discussed brings them together in a heightened form, and in a context which is more readily recognised as political than in some other cases discussed in other chapters.

For this case study we have drawn on published documents about particular programmes, on academic writing about the programmes, on our own direct experience in teaching in and researching such programmes and engaging in many discussions with teachers, students, policymakers and designers of such programmes. This is a 'case' that produced local examples across many countries and institutions over a sustained period. To illustrate the discussion here, we deliberately draw examples from a number of different countries (Canada, the UK, Denmark and Australia), and from different types of settings (technical colleges, adult education, tertiary teaching, professional courses) – but a wealth of other examples can be found.

Few things have put 'self-work' on the agenda in education and training as noticeably as the Women's Movement. Across most areas of adult and organisational education, and particularly in programmes educating teachers and trainers of various kinds, new programmes have been developed which *explicitly* embody the idea that one's gendered identity needs attention. Government policies, work-based initiatives, new courses in further, adult and higher education, all took up the idea that the old self, of both men and women, needed some reform. It had been producing undesirable outcomes, holding people back from their potential (in the case of women and careers) or oppressing people (by sexist assumptions in the case of male managers, or sexual harassers of various statuses). Gendered identity was seen as a core issue for pedagogical attention in the latter part of the twentieth century.

The new programmes concerned with gender take a variety of guises: re-entry or vocational programmes for women; 'Women's Studies' (or, more recently 'Men's Studies') courses in all sectors; workplace-based affirmative action training for people who sit on promotion committees or manage areas; and workplace sexual harassment training, to develop awareness of new legal obligations that govern workplace relationships. They take different forms and have differing ideologies, but in each case they explicitly make the participants in the class – students and teachers themselves – the subject of pedagogical scrutiny. Language, interpersonal style, dress, agendas and boundaries of 'private' and 'public', all become the subject of analysis and, often, of new regulation. In these programmes pedagogy is seen as a site for reform of the person and of social and work outcomes. Pedagogy and pedagogies of the self are seen as political acts, both by those promoting new directions and by those resisting or contesting them.

The area of gender reform is recognised by most people as a political activity and this explicitly political character differentiates it from most of the other cases discussed in this book. They are also political, engaged in an attempted reconstruction of identity to particular ends, but are not necessarily marked as such by those who engage in them. Although the programmes spawned by the movements around gender reform took voluntary (Women's Studies programmes, work opportunities for women etc.), compulsory ('equal opportunity train-ing' for people who were to serve on appointment and promotion committees) and punitive (programmes to correct sexual harassment, for example) forms, in this chapter we have primarily focused on voluntary programmes freely entered into by students. Readers might like to compare the technologies and narratives of the programmes discussed in this chapter with those of another voluntary programme aimed at self-improvement – the self-help books discussed in Chapter 4, a 'pedagogy' also designed to be 'freely' embarked on, but with a different narrative about what is holding the 'self' back, and a differ-ent, though at times overlapping, narrative of directions for recon-struction of identity.

Other interesting comparisons are with Chapter 6, on corporate training, and Chapter 7, on HIV/AIDS education. In relation to the question we posed in Chapters 1 and 2 ('What do pedagogies assume about the self?'), from the perspective of the case in this chapter, gender is a fundamental feature of identity, a key element of social situatedness and a central feature in 'reconstructing' a different future. In relation to the discussion of identity as narrative in Chapter 3, the programmes to be discussed here narrate gender as a central issue, both in terms of 'reflexive' (autobiographical) identity and in terms of 'relational' (social categorisation) identity. The perspective of this group of pedagogies assumes that programmes directed at producing change in relation to sexual behaviour (Chapter 7) or corporate be-haviour (Chapter 6) need to engage students as *gendered* subjects and engage with gender difference in their narratives of past and future self. And yet, the programmes discussed in those chapters, though temporally contiguous, and sometimes even working with the same people as their students, are both relatively silent about gender. In the corporate programmes, if it is addressed, it is likely to be as a marginal 'add on'. In the HOT game of Chapter 7, it is there but as one of a series of individual differences that are all simply that: indi-vidual preferences.

In another sense too, this chapter's case has a different character to many others we discuss: it is a site of pedagogical activity that has been the subject of very extensive reflexive theorisation by many people who have been participants in it. This work has fed lines of theoretical development that we discussed in the opening chapters of the book. Chapter 3 used as an illustration of one approach to teaching the anecdote 'we teach and they learn', and a similar stance is common in the writing of academic textbooks: 'we analyse, they practice; we see through, they just do' (see also Chapter 10).

Although writers identifying with a poststructural perspective, as discussed in Chapter 2, ostensibly are very self-reflexive and acutely aware of the contingent and constructed nature of their own claims to truth, it is still more common than not for poststructural texts about pedagogy to be ones where the expertise seems to be held by the writer and not by those they discuss (Yates 1992). In this chapter's case study, that is most evidently *not* the case. Here reflexivity and self-scrutiny are not only extensively practised by the pedagogues, but we can see the movement itself having a reflexive narrative over time. It is a useful reminder that in this book we are setting out to offer some approaches and ways of seeing to others who are similarly engaged in reflexively considering the form, processes and effects of pedagogical practices.

'The personal as political': consciousness raising as pedagogy

> Our admitted histories and contexts, when subjected to examination, can alter the form and content of how we learn and teach.
> (Culley *et al.* 1985: 19)

As a movement for change, the Women's Movement of the late twentieth century is often distinguished from what is called the 'first wave feminism' of the suffragette movement by its focus on issues of culture, representation and social relations ('sexism', 'femininity' and 'masculinity') as distinct from, or in addition to, legislative entitlements (rights, proscriptions). It was interested in how femininity and masculinity, female and male subjectivities came to take the form they do, and in exposing and changing some unfortunate consequences of then current forms.

By the middle of the twentieth century, women in western countries had the right to vote, and many measures of formal equality. What they discovered they didn't seem to have was equal power, or status, or recognised achievement. In some landmark books by de Beauvoir, Greer, Friedan and others, and in informal discussion groups that grew into associations such as the Women's Liberation Movement, the National Organization of Women in the USA and the Women's Electoral Lobby in Australia, the Women's Movement began to explore 'the problem that has no name' (sexism) and the ramifications of the idea that 'the personal is political' (that relations between husbands and wives, advertising images and popular culture, and even the very words we use, can maintain the power of some and the subordination of others). One strong image associated with the Movement (even if the extent of its reality as practice was highly exaggerated) was 'consciousness raising': that housewives and other like groups could come together and begin to discuss and share the dissatisfactions they felt, and by doing so could put words to processes and forms of inequality that were politically oppressive.

As pedagogical technologies, some of the key aspects of consciousness raising found fertile ground and a great deal of synchronicity with certain long-standing adult education practices (see Hart 1990 and Chapter 1). Adults, as many gurus of adult education proclaim, have something to bring to the educational exchange. They have their own experience, knowledge, expertise; they are capable of contributing to the direction of a discussion; of making decisions about what is important. Talk, group work, sharing, drawing on one's own experience are all grist to the mill of many humanist education practices, especially in continuing education.

The broad thrust of programmes influenced by a feminist conception of consciousness raising was that students (and often the teacher) would revisit their own experiences and learn to name and see these differently. This has many parallels to the Freirian idea of 'conscientisation' – Freire 1973 – which was also very popular with adult educators, especially adult literacy workers, and it is drawn on in the programme for youth workers discussed in Chapter 7. The pedagogical work was to find strategies which effected this revisiting and, especially, this renaming. We will first discuss three strategies that were common, and then go on to explore further issues that often emerged as tensions in these strategies.

Revisiting and sharing one's experiences

In class, in pairs, in small groups and to the whole group, students are asked to tell the story of their own life experiences, especially their own educational history and any critical or vivid incidents that are part of it. They are sometimes asked to produce more worked-up autobiographies as written texts; and in some classes, students are required to collaborate and act out each other's stories. The template story the students are being asked to produce is not necessarily made explicit, but it is one where unfortunate things have happened which the teller now regrets (e.g. a decision to leave school early, or to become a nurse, or to give up work to have children soon after they got married, or to work in an unrewarding job while their husbands did a higher degree). However, at the time, they regarded their decision as either natural and not contestable, or as an outcome of their own weakness. In the light of the course, the group discussions and associated readings, the teller is intended to discover that these incidents were not the result of inner failings but of ways of acting that had been socially built up and that could be changed (e.g. being accepting rather than assertive); or of social norms (especially in language) that should be unmasked and contested; or of individual or group male power that should also be challenged.

The process of self-work is meant to be one of *self-discovery*; but at the same time there is a particular kind of self-understanding and *reworking* to be discovered. Readers might note that this particular approach to 'reflecting on experience' does not neatly fit the assumptions of either of the models of this pedagogical strategy (by Brookfield 1991 and Gergen and Kaye 1992) outlined in Chapter 1. It does not assume, like Brookfield, that this is about uncovering a previously imperfectly understood inner self; nor, like Gergen and Kaye, that the agenda, the new identity, is to be seen simply as a series of possible language games. Like the critical pedagogy referred to in Chapter 1, it assumes a political shaping of identity in the past; it assumes that power and social critique are part of the technology of self-change. But it is not entirely untouched by the interests of those other models. More than earlier forms of critical pedagogy, it takes seriously the issue of emotions and feelings; it does not want to give up some sense of nurturing an inner self. And, the politics of gender have also meant that it treats more centrally issues of language and positioning. However, compared with Gergen and Kaye, the framing of this particular pedagogy generally retained some more modernist sensibilities in that some discursive positionings are considered to be more important than others, and there is an ongoing attention to a collective and not simply individual agenda for change.

Two further pedagogical strategies, commonly used in Women's Studies courses, helped set this reframing of identity on the right path.

The curriculum as a guide to 'who I am'

In most courses, in addition to sharing autobiographical accounts, students are encouraged or required to do a range of readings, and possibly viewings, of texts that examine lives from an appropriate political perspective: works on the feminine mystique and the female eunuch or on women's psychology and women's ways of knowing; novels such as *The Group* and *The Women's Room*; films and plays. This simultaneous attention to texts about other lives, and critical discussion of them, provides a backdrop of lessons to attune students to parallels that might be found in their own life. Some courses distribute a reading list in a conventional way, to be handed out on the first night of class. In others the teacher or lecturer aims to produce a more personalised curriculum for each student. In the first class (or the first few weeks of classes), students share experiences and 'discover' issues or problems that relate to their lives. The teacher or lecturer then guides them to books and articles that will allow them to analyse these problems and empower themselves.

Language: examining naming as construction

Most courses also spend some time considering language: the words we speak, the ways we speak, and the sexism and power embedded in these. Courses were asking students to look at naming practices: the ways women and men were addressed or addressed each other; the connotations of words used for women and for men; the types of themes men and women take up in conversation; and who does the interrupting (Tannen 1990 is a popular text).

The issue of gender and language is a particularly powerful intervention in classroom processes and a powerful technology to carry the revisiting and renaming of identity and experience being asked of students. Once introduced as a topic in a programme, it infiltrates all subsequent classes, and remains in students' perceptions and interactions outside the classroom. Focusing on the language we use, and on particular forms of interpersonal communication, is an evident way of accomplishing the work of disciplining the self, and the gaze of regulation is turned on the pedagogy and group as a whole.

The language issues here are related to but not identical with some other textual constructions of identity discussed in this book: the theory of identity as narrative discussed in Chapter 3 and the discussion of portfolio-based textual construction of the worker-learner in Chapter 5. In Chapter 3 we argued that constructions of identity involve a co-constructed relationship between 'reflexive' and 'relational' identifications. The questions gender reform grappled with were: What do the relational forms available for identity construction look like? Where do they come from? What produces change in available identities? For example, is it possible to produce a new available identity by simply coining or proscribing certain words (e.g. 'Ms') or outlawing demeaning or sexually identified descriptors? Or, do words need to follow other changes beyond textual practices if they are to be available as a reconstructed form of the self? Chapter 3 represented identity as an artefact of the characters, events and temporal sequences of narrative, but some popular theories of gendered identity emphasised a psychological and cognitive orientation on the part of gendered subjects that was not so readily manipulable. Tannen's work, for example, argued that gendered ways of reasoning could not be easily replaced by new narratives of the self, but that these narratives of difference could be understood and negotiated in new ways. The work on gender and language also raised some issues about embodiment as a limitation to narrative reconstructions of self. For example, if practices are changed, if a new identity is claimed (e.g. assertiveness by a woman; or a self-deprecating, modest and sensitive approach by a man seeking promotion), this may work to reconstruct identity – or it may serve to illustrate instead the point made in Chapter 3, that not all identities are open to all.

Constructing the pedagogical subject

The learner in the types of Women's Studies programmes outlined here is assumed to be a (potentially) rational subject – one who is not bound to be blinded by social ideology, but potentially, through reading, discussion and sharing, able to critique and change their view of who they have been. In this sense, they fit the imputed subject of critical pedagogy programmes discussed in Chapter 1. They are also assumed to be very much formed in discourse, and changing language is seen as a central mechanism of changing the person. But the learners are also assumed to have a commonality, to share, in at least some senses, a common experience and a common 'oppression' – learning to discover what is common about the experience and identity they hold, and to see this as social, not simply innate, is an important part of the foundation of consciousness raising.

Problems of difference and resistance

For consciousness raising (or indeed for 'conscientisation') the *composition* of the class is a problematic agenda. The issues to be revisited and politicised here are not 'academic' (in the sense of that phrase 'an academic question' – not a question of the angels on pinheads variety). They touch on deep emotions and deeply-held beliefs about one's personal relationships and indeed who one is (or was). Any disagreements in values, naming or life choices are likely to be felt as personal criticism, to be deeply wounding and to threaten the group process:

> One method of dealing with self-hate engendered by a misogynist and racist culture can be to direct negative feelings toward other women, other people of color, and the classroom offers opportunity for this behavior. Students tend to categorize each other and may turn on each other – the 'women's libber' on the one always mentioning 'my boyfriend'; the one who comes to class in jeans and a sweat shirt on the one with heavy make-up and a different skirt every day; the lower-class woman on the one she perceives as privileged. Male students, often uneasy and uncomfortable, can sometimes strike out in extreme responses.
>
> (Culley 1985: 213)

One strategy is to develop 'woman only' courses (or men's groups). But even in groups formed on a relatively natural and like-minded basis (such as the Women's Neighbourhood Houses in Australia), the fine differences of personal choices and of political values can be a considerable problem. Larger differences can emerge on a global as well as local front in relation to race and ethnicity.

In the 1970s and 1980s, a good deal of the emphasis in courses of the women-only and consciousness raising variety was on a common type of self to be discovered; one which had suffered from sexist practices, one which had 'women's ways of knowing' rather than the 'masculine' forms education had taken for granted. The self-work, the directions in which the self was to be scrutinised and recast, also emphasised some common forms: learning to become more 'autonomous', more assertive, to reject naming practices and domestic relations that assumed a non-equality between women and men, husband and wife. The strategy was premised on seeing the classroom as an *inclusive* space, where women could now speak and discover who they were and what they wanted. But the debates around race showed that many women experienced this space as not inclusive of their own particular experience, particularly if their experience had been of a minority ethnic or racial group, in which their family was a source of comfort in a racist world. They did not recognise themselves in the template identity to be worked on. But the teachers or facilitators were committed to inclusiveness, and wanted to acknowledge and work with these testimonies too, not to ignore them.

One result of these debates is that the technology of consciousness raising, of addressing and reworking the self, now has to try to incorporate both difference and commonality. In some cases this has led to the work on the self becoming much more theoretically governed (many course reading lists now grow heavier with references to Foucault, Spivak, Judith Butler and others) with balances shifting between sharing and high theory, and many debates inside and outside class about whether work on gender is moving too far away from the direct engagements with which it began (Yates 1993; McLeod *et al.* 1994).

There is also a greater recognition that the strategy of working on the self through sharing testimony of personal experiences produces difficult political and emotional resonances in the classroom for the teacher, trainer or facilitator. This in turn brings new attention to the identity of the teacher or lecturer. They too have to subject themselves to pedagogical techniques: they are required to be reflexive, to scrutinise themselves and to engage in self-work in the course of their pedagogy.

Here are two of the many examples of such discussions. Amy Rossiter (1997) discusses the problems she feels as a social work lecturer in a Canadian university, trying to introduce a new critical consciousness, yet working in an institutional context which regulates pedagogy to take conventional markers of achievement, and in which teachers' authority is often seen by students to be in ratio to their demonstrated professional competence (a function of the extent that they are known to be a good social worker or teacher or nurse themselves). The issue of considering education as a site for reproduction/ conformity or as a site for transcendence or revolution is not new. What is interesting here is the way this is now seen as an issue about the identity and subjectivity of the *teacher*, as an issue about what sorts of selves are being brought to the classroom, and about how these come together in the exchanges of teachers and students in particular institutional contexts: 'I am interested in the difficulties academics face in terms of subjectivities as teachers, particularly those of us who teach in professional disciplines like social work, education or nursing' (Rossiter 1997: 29). Rossiter begins by discussing the fact that although there is a wealth of material on dealing with the 'diverse classroom',

These new technologies fail me as I watch the totally puzzled face of my Ethiopian student who was recently released from years of torture and beatings in jail, as she tries to hear my explanation of Foucault's ideas on the capillary nature of power . . . Such moments are profound challenges to my own identity.

(1997: 30)

Rossiter describes the way she tries to work given that she is working with such Foucauldian perspectives on governmentality (as discussed in Chapter 2): she recognises that university structures, assessment practices and evaluations of teaching embody a disciplinary gaze, mechanisms of control and an imperative to regulation of the self: 'The question frequently thrown up as the ultimate challenge is "how do you know they're getting it?" . . . When I comply with this definition of teaching, I produce compliance, so that a double regulation of myself and my students is effected' (1997: 32). Rossiter's own attempts to be transformational, to have the students see issues of race, class and gender in their practices, use many of the familiar techniques of such classrooms. Students are asked to write a journal about the experience of interviewing each other; they are asked to talk about their values with each other and with the teacher; and so on. Rossiter not only complies with the institutional requirements of self-scrutiny in the form of producing teaching evaluations, course materials and so on, but also produced a further layer of self-scrutiny in the form of a conference paper and later a journal article for those who shared her concerns.

Kate McKenna, in another self-reflection produced for the same audiences, takes up the theme of 'dealing with difference differently'. Speaking of the emotions and investments she has seen in highly charged classroom discussions, she writes:

I find it astounding that in academic pedagogical interactions participants continue to treat as 'ordinary', forms of communication by groups which if they were exhibited by 'an individual', would leave him or her in grave danger of being diagnosed under a variety of psychiatric categories.

(McKenna 1997: 50)

She goes on to argue for foregrounding in the curriculum what has previously been the subtext of these classrooms: the histories that have led the diverse students and teachers to be the way they are, and to be positioned the way they are, and the emotional investments they exhibit in the classroom. Like our book, McKenna sees the emotions and the pedagogies of the teacher-learner exchange not as a personal and private matter, but as social and cultural products, and she engages in a project where she interviews different teachers about critical moments in their teaching that they then subject to self-scrutiny.

Many of the examples produced by teachers interviewed by McKenna[1] are about how a teacher might act in relation to students who explicitly oppose the direction of the change and self-work the teacher is concerned with. Incidents reported to McKenna included female students who resisted being taught about social transformation by a male lecturer; a class of students who resisted a teacher who asked them to look at racism and colonialism in an assignment; a male student who proclaimed that sometimes women deserve to be beaten; a gay student who complained about the classroom that overtly asked for participation and speech but in its processes produced silence about the issues he wanted to talk about. McKenna's conclusion, like many similar teachers, is to advocate that classes engage centrally in the study of subjectivity, so that teachers and students can all acquire greater reflexivity about who they are, and can see the issues of gender, race and class they are enmeshed in or help to perpetuate:

> Shifting this [the problem that people can't hear each other] would require a self-reflexivity in which the reader/listener's present emotional/conceptual responses would be de-naturalised through an exploration of the ways these responses enact particular histories in the present, examining how the past continues as an active force that is shaping current life, including one's (in)capacities for engagement with the radical alterity of the other . . . The historical refashioning must include the (counter) transference of frameworks that may prevent educators, researchers, students and communities from noticing things . . .
>
> (McKenna 1997: 65)

Technologies of collaborative self-inquiry and the problem of authority

Pedagogical strategies that are about sharing, inclusiveness and self-scrutiny, but that stem from political movements, inevitably run into problems at the point where decisions are made about who holds the floor; what directions of scrutiny are sanctioned or not sanctioned; and, especially, what are the criteria by which students' work or participation is assessed.

Courses designed to 'interrupt gender' through mechanisms of individual and collective self-scrutiny produce many fiery moments for teachers because they so clearly make pedagogy and power, and the actions of the teacher, a legitimate subject for classroom scrutiny and talk. In some senses they legitimise (or normalise) objections to the teacher and to the pedagogy. As we discussed above in relation to the technology of consciousness raising, the use of books, films and templates as well as group processes provides some direction to self-scrutiny, some implicit desirable outcome regarding the messages and new identities to be discovered by the students. But it is also part of the movement that is the case study of this particular chapter that the teachers themselves in such courses frequently identify with the 'oppressed' whose story they are trying to reveal. They feel hurt but also relatively powerless in the face of students who insist on not hearing these messages, who resist the critical scrutiny of self that is often practised more strongly by the teacher than by any student in the class, as the previous section illustrated. Students can and do resist the pedagogies of the classroom in many ways: by voting with their feet and abandoning the subject; by ridiculing the teacher; by forming alliances and subverting the agenda (e.g. insisting that to be consistent the teacher should give up their role and authority). At the same time, further waves of self-scrutiny are generated by the teachers or 'victims' of these practices: they write articles about them; theorise them; revisit their practices and their theories.

In terms of assessment, many teachers of such courses produce their own individual acts of rebellion against institutional forms (e.g. one lecturer gave all her students an 'A'; others simply refused to provide grades). But for those who do not see this as an option, who work in courses in institutional contexts, who are prepared to comply at least minimally with assessment of students on a pass/fail basis, the issue is what is being assessed? If formal essays are set, they commonly ask not just that the students demonstrate their understanding of particular literature or arguments, but that they demonstrate that they can apply these to their own biography or situation. Chapter 5 provides a comparative example which discusses how work-based learning portfolios require a different type of textual construction of identity. Sometimes in classes on gender the only requirement is participation itself: that the students produce an oral testimony in class, that they demonstrate that they have kept a journal, that they do participate in scrutinising themselves and each other. Here the *process* of working on the self is given priority over the acquisition of any particular knowledge about the self.

The technologies of self discussed above are one form of the 'reflection on experience' discussed in Chapter 1, often found in adult education courses, both formal and institutional, but brought to a heightened form in many women's studies contexts. We turn next to courses with a more central vocational and pragmatic agenda: how do courses in this area construct identity in relation to gender, change and desirable outcomes?

Vocational courses as pedagogies of the (gendered) self

In many countries, movements to change educational provision for women followed recognition of statistics that women entered a much narrower range of jobs than men, and ended up through their adult life with lower pay, lower job security and worse opportunities for advancement. New provisions and policies aimed to broaden women's opportunities but, from the beginning, they recognised that this task was a dual one: one part of it was to provide education or training about the vocational field or skills in question; the other was to somehow engage the potential and actual students so that they would see new vocational directions as not incompatible with 'who they were'.

In 1996, for example, the National Institute of Adult Continuing Education in the UK published a booklet reporting details of over 70 programmes that had been submitted for an award to recognise 'Good Practice in Women's Education and Training' (Coats 1996). The editor notes that the six awards made constitute a range 'that recognises diversity and responds to difference', clearly marking this as a publication of the 1990s rather than one of two decades earlier. But she is pleased that although changes in European Union (EU) and UK policies have now produced a mandatory emphasis on certification or qualifications and vocational skill outputs, some self-work continues to be a feature of good practice for women in vocational education and training:

> the essential component of a course that provided women with a chance to discover, in a supportive group, what their interests and potential might be, remains an important part of the overall

provision for women. Despite the emphasis on vocational input and the need for accreditation, it was heartening to find that a number of the submissions retained the key elements of this kind of provision.

(Coats 1996: 85)

Coats' booklet provides summaries of 70 different courses being conducted in different parts of the UK, and these give the reader a quick overview of what components are considered appropriate in a vocational training course for women. South Leeds Open Learning Centre, for example, includes the following components in its programme. We have put in italics the elements that directly address the need to work on the self or identity:

Core programme:

- Basic IT awareness
- *Team leadership/supervisory skills*
- *Wider opportunities and job search skills*
- Health, safety and emergency aid at work
- *Confidence-building and assertiveness*
- *Communication skills*
- *Psychology of work/women and power*

With options in:

- *Introduction to caring*
- European language taster
- *Art and design*
- Work experience
- *Creative writing*
- *Residential week at Northern College – 'Women in Society'*
- Brush up your skills – maths and English workshop.

(Coats 1996: 23)

Llandrillo College in Wales describes its own programme for women who wish to re-enter the labour market. And again, the emphasis in italics has been added by us:

Due to the types of job that have traditionally been available to women – service industries, the retail trade and caring sectors – women have suffered both horizontal and vertical occupational segregation. In an attempt to redress this balance the course has *a high content of personal development* aimed at improving women's *self-image* and *teaching them to aspire*. It seeks to *empower participants to make better choices about their futures* by enabling them *to become better choosers*. The course also aims to provide women with both generic and specific skills to meet the needs of a changing economy . . .

(Coats 1996: 26)

This programme description constructs learner identities (i.e. of women who have been out of the workforce for a long time) as emotionally bounded and requiring support. It sees such women as experiencing problems 'when the time comes to reassess their lives', including 'lack of confidence, a loss of self-belief and a sense of isolation'. Quite fundamental forms of self-work are recognised here as important for women who want to be in paid work. They not only need more confidence and skill, they also need to 'learn to aspire', to 'learn to be better choosers'. A different identity is needed. It is interesting to compare this agenda with the discussion of the self-help literature in Chapter 4. There is some commonality in the desirable identity set up in both cases: the successful worker of western capitalism. But the manuals set up this identity as an authentic self to be 'uncovered', albeit also requiring learning particular narratives of self, and requiring training in certain new habits. The vocational courses here take up a different idea: that for women to be the successful worker identity of western capitalism, they need to be different from how women have been in the past. The task is not uncovering an 'authentic' self, but constructing a more fulfilling identity. It is not good enough to let learners assume that they know what they need; forming in them an 'enlarged' perspective on who they are and what they need is part of the pedagogical agenda:

> We believe there is a balance to be struck between recognising the importance of listening to what women say they want and recognising that women may express needs on the basis of limited information. Too close a reliance on responding to expressed need therefore will make us ineffective in our role of enlarging that range of opportunities open to women.
>
> (Coats 1996: 121)

This programme also seeks to improve women as choosers, and is piloting an introductory module that 'would give women the opportunity to analyse how they came to make decisions about what they would like to learn, what style of learning suits them best, and alternative pathways and directions they could explore as adult learners'.

In terms of technologies of pedagogy, the self-work for women in vocational programmes, especially those involving re-entry, commonly involves a combination of some consciousness raising regarding work and inequalities, as discussed in the previous section – this is where they 'learn to aspire' – and some deliberate inculcation of traits seen to be associated with the successful male worker – particularly confidence and assertiveness.

An Australian programme to produce 'gender inclusive teaching' in technical and further education indicates that in the vocational area, just as in the more general Women's Studies arena discussed in the previous section, 'self-work' is expected to extend to the teachers, not just their students:

> What is needed then is a professional development program which is concerned with assisting teachers to analyse their attitudes to gender. Where these attitudes have a constraining effect on a particular group of students, i.e. women, the program should assist the teachers to change their behaviour to provide an enabling environment for all students.
>
> (Australia DEET undated: 32)

Another example that points to ways in which vocational preparation *is* identity work, and, as such, open to resistance by students, is seen in Denmark in a context where unemployed men are required to undertake retraining. Retraining people whose jobs have disappeared is now seen as requiring some identity work – they need to learn to become different types of people. The problem uncovered by researchers and teachers is that those designated by policymakers as most in need of retraining and further education (unemployed men) are least likely to want to engage in it. Thus 'there was a need of having a deeper look into the motivations, possibilities and barriers related to mature unskilled workers' educational chances' (Hansen 2000: 573). The preliminary research suggests that the group which from some perspectives is now doing worst out of contemporary forms of the labour market (working-class men) are most resistant to the type of self-work considered necessary to improve their job chances.

The field of vocational education for women and men today brings together two areas which have highlighted the issue of the self as an arena for work: the contemporary rethinking of gender and the contemporary reshaping of what 'work' is. From feminism and Gender Studies came a movement that resisted many previous views of the individual's personality and traits, abilities and aspirations as being innate or natural, as something that might be taken for granted or treated as a given in the work of pedagogy. The new pedagogies of gender reform emphasised rather their socially constructed character and set in train a wide range of investigations and strategies to scrutinise and reform not only people's 'rational' knowledge and aspirations, but their very emotional investments in who they were and what they wanted. New moves to scrutinise, regulate and dis-cipline the self are carried not just by state mandate and reform policies (though in part these new moves were taking up capitalist values and simply asking that these be spread more widely), but also developed from a political movement that saw itself as trying to change social outcomes. In this movement, the agendas and pedagogies of self-work form an ongoing spiral, interweaving teaching practice, teacher reflections, political movements and research theories in the academy.

At the same time, as we all keep being told, the nature of work has changed (see e.g. du Gay 1996a; Gee 2000; Boud and Solomon 2001b and Chapters 5 and 6). In the twenty-first century, self-scrutiny and the type of self or identity that is offered is recognised as a vocational issue, not just as something that relates to the job interview. Work skills are not seen as competencies that may be possessed or lacking, as things that do not touch on the inner person. Rather, the discussion of lifelong and flexible learning assumes that orientations of the self are inseparable from the successful acquisition and demonstration of competency. Old ideas of what is open for 'public' scrutiny (e.g. work skills) and what is properly 'private' (e.g. personal values; how a husband and wife divide up their domestic life) have been changed and so have educational ideas about what is 'natural' and what is constructed and open to change in learners. Discursive reconstructions of identity are recognisably part of work preparation pedagogy.

Concluding comments

In this chapter we have taken for examination pedagogies of gender-based change which take multiple local forms, some of which are likely to be familiar to most readers. We have tried to draw attention to the particular technologies associated with them, some directions they have taken and some problems they have encountered, not least in relation to the putative learner subject not neatly fitting the model subject of the pedagogy. Discursive, textual and narrative reconstructions of identity are an important tool of the pedagogies described in this chapter. The developments here both illustrate and disrupt a number of the models and theories discussed in our first two chapters.

In relation to Chapter 1 and different education traditions of self-work, what is noticeable is that even though two of the examples discussed at length in this chapter (consciousness raising, and vocational programmes) might seem initially to fit the historical distinction in programmes of adult education between those that are psychological and humanist in foundation, and those that are sociological and critical in their conception of the human subject, the feminist agenda was to insist that the two needed to be brought together. A central issue for the pedagogy was one that might be seen as a development of humanist traditions: what makes women students comfortable? What are their preferred 'ways of knowing'? What conditions allow them to speak? But a critical and more sociologically oriented perspective was also the starting point: a sense that language, jobs and the division of labour had structured who we were, and that this now needed to be uncovered and changed. As the outline of courses for women returning to work discussed in this chapter clearly indicates, the distinction in content and process between programmes designed for 'empowerment' of the learner and those designed to produce a skilled worker is less clear-cut than in many previous traditions of vocational and adult education.

In relation to Chapter 2 and its discussion of theories of a unified rational self versus theories of a multiple dynamic self, the gender pedagogies sit uneasily on either single side of this binary: they believe in a self that is constructed and reconstructable, take seriously multiple positionings and their effects, especially in the workplace, but are less willing to see students and possibilities as simply the sum of their discursive positionings. The embodied person, psychology, emotions, confidence and gendered ways of knowing feature strongly in the conception of how pedagogy should function, and in terms of to what ends it should be functioning.

Again, further to the discussion in Chapter 2 of the influential Foucauldian concept of governmentality in relation to identity, the case discussed in this chapter is interesting. Courses designed to explore the gendered subject were often attempting to work with some version of these concepts: to understand students and teachers, and pedagogy itself, in terms of governmentality. But the imperatives of the teachers and programme-initiators involved in these courses can equally, simultaneously, be read as a continued commitment to a more modernist project of change. The reflections by Amy Rossiter earlier in this chapter nicely illustrate the dilemmas teachers experience in trying to work both within and against governmentality.

Note

1 Other interesting related discussions include Lewis and Simon 1986; Ellsworth 1989; and Luke and Gore 1992.

Chapter 9

Educational programmes for sex offenders

Correcting oneself

Introduction

Sex offender education provides a site for the exploration of a range of issues relating to the role of education in personal change. It is particularly interesting because of its location with respect to a number of established and entrenched boundaries: professional boundaries (e.g. prison officers, welfare workers, educators); disciplinary boundaries (e.g. psychology, social science, education); boundaries between prison and the community, educational compulsion and choice, perpetrators and victims, punitive justice and restorative justice, treatment and education; and boundaries between facilitators and penal enforcers. Although there are the inevitable tensions and ambiguities associated with operating in a highly contested space, they are rendered invisible by the single-minded purpose of sex offender education: the reduction or prevention of reoffending. This chapter focuses on material generated by two primary sources: a comparative study of sex offender management practices (Lundstrom 2002), and curriculum materials developed by the Center for Sex Offender Management (CSOM 2002). Lundstrom's report compares sex offender management practices in Ireland, the UK, Vermont and Canada. She also reports on interviews conducted with a range of stakeholders within the Irish prison system, including sex offenders, prison officers, prison managers, prison educators, specialist services staff and administrative staff.

The chapter aims to illuminate the way in which conventional teacher and learner identities are disrupted and problematised, first by the broader context of sex offender education and second by teacher training and treatment/education interventions. In contrast to the other case studies in this book our primary focus is on teacher identities and how such identities are assumed, shaped or constrained by the pedagogy of teacher training. In this instance we rely solely on how the text of a particular teacher training manual positions the teacher. We also suggest that commonly held beliefs about what constitutes 'good' teaching and the role of the teacher (and learner) are problematised by the broader context of sex offender education – i.e. the institutional management of sex offenders (e.g. stated purposes of the criminal justice system); the need to position oneself as a 'teacher' within a continuum of offender containment, surveillance, measurement and therapy; and the multidisciplinary nature of sex offender management (e.g. the role of education in relation to other professionals such as psychologists, prison officers, social workers).

This chapter is thus primarily concerned with the way in which teachers in sex offender education programmes are subjected to a great deal of self-work, and how they in turn need to engage with issues relating to their identity.

Contextual issues in the management of sex offenders

An important aspect of teacher identity is how they position themselves in relation to broad social purposes. This is particularly salient with sex offender education because of the contestation around the 'broader social purpose' in managing sex offenders. In this regard it is important to note that the management of sex offenders differs quite markedly in different jurisdictions, and it is strongly influenced by the values informing any particular criminal justice system. Lundstrom (2002) provides a good map of some of the issues. For example, she points out the difference between subscribing to a punitive one, as opposed to a restorative one, and how this affects all aspects of the management of sex offenders. Quite clearly an educational programme informed by the concept of restorative justice is very different from one informed by the concept of punitive justice. For a start, education is seen as more significant under a restorative justice regime with its focus on interventions that control or reduce an offender's risk of reoffending. This can be illustrated by taking a more detailed look at the differences between the concepts of restorative and punitive justice, the contrasting features of which are set out below (Lundstrom 2002: 77).

Features of a punitive justice system:

- Victim ignored, offender passive
- Crime defined as a violation of the state

- Focus on establishing blame, on guilt, on past
- Adversarial relationships and process normative
- One social injury replaced by another
- Community on sideline, represented abstractly by state
- Action directed from state to offender
- Offence defined in purely legal terms, devoid of moral, social, economic, political dimensions.

Features of a restorative justice system:

- Victim rights/needs recognised, offender encouragement to take responsibility
- Crime defined as violation of one person by another
- Focus on problem solving, on liabilities and obligations, on future (what should be done?)
- Dialogue and negotiation normative
- Focus on repair of social injury
- Community as facilitator in restorative process
- Offender accountability defined as understanding impact of action and helping decide how to make things right
- Offence understood in whole context – moral, social, economic and political.

In a restorative justice system, educators are seen as sitting along-side a continuum of professionals delivering a service in an inclusive 'case management' approach. Such professionals include probation and parole officers, casework supervisors, community correctional officers and volunteers. Indeed, all these roles could be seen as having an educational dimension. Implied under the restorative justice banner is a certain position or posture for the teacher: it is the teacher as mediator between the victim, the community and the offender. It is the teacher who adopts inclusive educational practices and who models the processes of dialogue, negotiation and mutuality. In such a scenario a teacher would be expected to adopt reflective pedagogical practices, to highlight interpersonal relations and empathy, and to keep the victim visible in the educational process. A restorative approach allows for a different way of thinking about things (largely because both sides are participants) and different kinds of identities for offenders and teachers.

In contrast, teachers who align with a punitive justice ethic are more likely to position themselves as 'knowers' who have access to the 'right' attitudes, behaviours and values, and can inculcate these in the learners on behalf of the state. The learners are objects of discipline and the educational process is aimed at transmitting the right way of being.

It should be noted that these polar positions are played out in the media and they help to produce available identities which can be taken up by offenders and educators, teachers and managers (see the discussion of this in Chapter 3).

It would be naive to assume that teachers align themselves in an unreflective way with prevailing institutional or official views about the broader purposes of the criminal justice system. Indeed, it is the highly contested nature of the terrain that presents particular difficulties for how teachers position themselves and are positioned. This is particularly evident in the struggle to negotiate the nature of the teacher-learner relationship in this setting.

Teacher-learner relationships

As discussed in Chapter 1, in most educational settings the nature of the teacher-learner relationship is an enactment of political, psychological and philosophical positions. From a psychological point of view interpersonal relationships are likely to be emotionally charged, as manifested in the different attitudes, expectations and actions of teachers and learners towards each other. This general state of affairs is particularly pertinent to sex offender education, largely because of the conflicting and emotionally charged views and attitudes of the stakeholders, but also because education is positioned within (or along-side) therapeutic and containment/surveillance interventions.

But perhaps the most significant characteristic of sex offender education, at least as far as teacher-learner relationships are concerned, is that the majority of offenders are men and many of the teachers are women. This presents particular issues for female teachers or facilitators, as expressed by one respondent:

> For a woman facilitator there are issues over power. Sex offenders have distorted attitudes to women. The woman team member should be clear about her position on the team in terms of power. She should be seen as an equal professional team member which should be modelled for the offenders. She should portray the professional me as opposed to the feminine me.
>
> (Lundstrom 2002: 28)

Another respondent refers to the prevailing attitude to women in prisons: 'In prison there is a male attitude that women have to be protected from "nastiness". There are apologies for bad language. There is also the impression that sex offending is a dirty area that women should not really get involved in' (Lundstrom 2002: 27). Many report that offenders often 'test' the teacher with the expression of extreme opinions about violence against women or explicit sexual talk which is designed to undermine and challenge the authority and position of the teacher. Others report having to deal with unwanted compliments from sex offenders.

Finding a comfortable posture as a teacher in this context involves quite a challenge, one which no doubt problematises commonly accepted conceptions of 'good' teaching practice (such as having a high regard for learners, attempting to see the world from their perspective, validating learners' experiences and so on). In Lundstrom's study one teacher remarked on the contradictory need to both 'confront' the offenders and their offence, and to provide a 'safe' environment for learning. Others reported the need for a non-judgemental posture which neither condemns nor condones the offence, as in the following testimony: 'A person's behaviours should be separated from the person themselves. One should never focus on the individual's offence at all unless the focus comes from themselves' (Lundstrom 2002: 29). Still others report on the need to defend sex offenders from unwarranted hostility:

> It is amazing the amount of hostility shown towards sex offenders in prison. They are called all sorts of names, 'the hairies' and this and that. Yet someone who would have battered old people over the head and robbed their life savings and left them for dead are not considered so dreadful. There are ultra negative attitudes towards sex offenders and it has to stop.
>
> (Lundstrom 2002: 29)

These different postures taken up by teachers (a confronting/challenging posture, a non-judgemental posture or an advocacy posture) illustrate the complexity and contradictory nature of the teacher's role in this setting. It is a setting where the politics of incarceration come up against sexual politics, where interpersonal relationships between teachers and learners are heavily inflected, and where a teacher's alignment with a given educational 'tradition' is likely to be compromised.

Teacher 'qualities'

Commonly endorsed teacher qualities such as 'accepting', 'facilitating', 'empathising', 'validating' and being 'learner centred' are problematised in significant ways by teacher training regimes for sex offender educators. This is well illustrated by examining extracts from the CSOM *Training Curriculum*. Section 5 is entitled 'Practical Supervision Strategies'. Among the 11 areas covered are 'desensitisation' and 'maintaining control of interactions with offenders'. The very idea of teachers being 'desensitised' is certainly contrary to the spirit of most teacher education programmes. The text for the presentation of the 'desensitisation topic' reads as follows:

> Sensitivity is a term in good currency today. We hear much about sensitivity training and how important it is to be sensitive to any number of issues and individuals. However, experienced probation/parole officers advise that to work with sex offenders, it is important to 'desensitize' oneself to some degree. Offenders have often engaged in unspeakable behavior that has created life-altering trauma for their victims. Their behavior can be so far beyond the boundaries of civilized human interaction that we are naturally appalled. In the words of a seasoned parole officer who has supervised sex offenders for many years, a supervising probation/parole agent must deal with sex offenders 'in a non-judgemental way . . . you have to temporarily suspend disbelief and set aside the normal revulsion that we might have for these offenders' behavior'. This may seem counter to an individual's sense of right and wrong, but probation/parole officers emphasize that it is necessary to suspend judgment to allow oneself to function effectively as a supervision officer. Suspending judgment of the person does not mean losing sight of the fact that the persons' behavior is not acceptable, is illegal, and is harmful to victims.
>
> (CSOM 2002: 3)

A technique for desensitisation includes the following :

> Deliberately adopting a neutral tone and demeanor during your interactions with the offender, fully anticipating that some disclosure or discussion of the details of the offense may be quite unsettling. One neutral reaction technique is to respond by saying,

'let me write that down', which breaks eye contact, gives you focus for your attention, and offers a neutral, routine response.

(CSOM 2002: 3–4)

How different this is to Rogers' (1983) influential ideas on the core qualities of the 'good' facilitator: realness and genuineness (entering into a relationship with learners which is personal rather than based on the prescribed role of the teacher); prizing, acceptance, trust (a caring for and confidence in the learner as a person of worth); empathic understanding (the capacity to understand the learner's perspective at both an intellectual and emotional level in a non-evaluative, accepting way).

A second topic in the CSOM programme is 'Maintaining Control of Interactions with Offenders', which has the following text: 'Realizing that sex offenders are often experts in manipulation and deception, it is critically important for the probation/parole officer to develop strategies to maintain control of all interactions and to develop rapport with the offender' (CSOM 2002: 5–6). The strategies include:

- Establishing your competence and knowledge
- Using a neutral tone of voice
- Establishing and holding the offender to standards of dress and/ or behaviour
- Setting and maintaining boundaries.

Sex offenders will often attempt to create inappropriate relationships with their supervising officers. They may proffer gifts, notes, or letters; ask about an officer's personal and family life; or try to establish themselves as 'special' . . . strategies to combat these attempts to manipulate one's boundaries are fairly straightforward. Some probation/parole officers report that they do not have personal items in their offices. They do not divulge information about themselves or their families in the context of a meeting with an offender. They decline gifts and correspondence, emphasizing that they are inappropriate. They do not let small behaviors go unaddressed and they respond to attempts at manipulation or deceit, no matter how small or insignificant, with statements such as 'this is what you are attempting to do and it is not appropriate because . . .'

(CSOM 2002: 7)

This kind of advice constitutes a defence against the presumed manipulations of learners. It acknowledges that the roles of teacher and learner are highly contested, as revealed in the conflicting attitudes, expectations and actions of teachers and learners towards each other. It constitutes a counter to the humanistic tradition, which has been cast as essentially 'feminine' in character, especially with its emphasis on feelings, caring and nurturance (Williams 1993). And, rather ironically, it is ultimately dehumanising and counter to prevailing beliefs about what constitutes a 'good citizen'.

Notwithstanding the above examples, the CSOM training does involve some exploration of empathy for the sex offender, as illustrated by the following exercise from Section 3:

> Take out a piece of paper (pause)
>
> Now write down a description of your first sexual experience. After you do this, I will ask you to share what you have written with someone else in the room.
>   Stop. What was going through your mind? The point here is not to do the writing or the sharing, but to think about how it felt to be asked to reveal ourselves and talk about our sexuality. It's important to keep those feelings in mind as we approach sex offenders with these questions – in terms of both our own level of comfort or discomfort and the offender's.
>
>   (CSOM 2002: 22)

(Participants are told not to follow the instructions – the exercise is really to surface the feelings aroused in the anticipation of doing the exercise.)

This is a most interesting exercise, with its own version of 'coitus interruptus' as it were. Significantly the exercise does not (necessarily) invite the participant to empathise with the offender's deviant sexuality, but rather with the feelings of comfort or discomfort the offender may have in discussing their sexuality. Even so, it stands in stark contrast to the desensitisation and 'control' exercises referred to above and the cyborg-like prescriptions for the 'ideal' sex offender educator/manager as described in the following edited list of desired characteristics (CSOM 2002: 17):

- Able to set limits with clients
- Comfortable confronting clients and holding them accountable for their behavior

- Comfortable discussing sex
- Comfortable with his or her own sexuality
- Good relationships with men and women
- Good self-esteem
- Comfortable working with sex offenders and their offense behavior
- Comfortable challenging distorted views of men and women
- Willing to work without developing a trusting relationship with the client
- Does not need acceptance from clients
- Comfortable with involuntary clients
- Able to cope with stress
- Able to maintain objectivity.

This list constitutes a 'profile' of the ideal sex offender educator. As such it reinforces the general point that the positioning of teachers in this site demands a great deal of self-work. It is self-work towards a singular, perfect person with stable psychological characteristics. Compared with similar teacher training manuals in other contexts there is a great deal of attention devoted to constructing the teacher. The list (in combination with the other material above) also says a great deal about offenders and the presumed dynamics of their 'change'. How then is the offender positioned?

Offender/learners' characteristics

Offenders too are seen as having a number of common psychological attributes, despite the inevitable diversity in the sex offences committed (not to mention the historical and cultural differences in what constitutes a sex offence). Two broad constructions of the sex offender are apparent: the offender has been overwhelmed by uncontrolled desires and distorted sexual drives (the psychodynamic subject), and the offender as having a set of characteristics which can be measured, calibrated and altered, in much the same way as a tailor alters a garment (the calculable subject).

The psychodynamic subject

The teacher training material cited above, which is largely designed to provide psychological protection for the teacher, assumes a highly motivated, psychodynamic subject 'equipped with an internal dynamic orientation to the world, with needs to be shaped and satisfied' and 'driven by unconscious forces and conflicts' (Rose 1996: 65). But there is an assumption that change is likely to be resisted by offenders and that every attempt will be made to manipulate and undermine the teacher. Furthermore, the view advanced is that trust and acceptance of others is not a precondition of learning and personal change.

It is interesting then to compare this material with the documentation of offenders' views about needed improvements in the sex offender programmes in the Irish prison system (Lundstrom 2002). What are noted in the report as some of the offenders' perceptions of how programmes could be improved are:

- The programme should be available to offenders when they request it and they should not have to apply several times.
- The start of the programme is too abrupt and nerve-racking; there is a need for the men to get comfortable and build up trust with one another. As one offender put it: 'There is a need to build up the person's self-esteem before looking at the dark side of his personality'.
- There should be time to talk to programme facilitators.
- The victim empathy module should be given more time, especially the contributions from the Rape Crisis Centre and Temple Street Children's Hospital. Offenders considered the input was excellent and the impact horrific.
- There should be time to 'come down' after a session.
- There should be an aftercare programme putting emphasis on practical things one could do in real situations to prevent reoffending
- There should be a good mix of different categories of offenders on a programme so that the proceedings do not get dominated by any one offence type (e.g. rapists or paedophiles).
- There should be an anger management programme.
- Core modules should focus on such issues as addiction, employment, general intimacy, occupational skills, offending behaviour, social skills, suicide, violence/anger and personal victimisations.

Here we have an emphasis on access, trust, empathy, communication and the need to attend to emotions (e.g. anger management and 'coming down') and develop interpersonal skills. There is also an implied resistance to the generic label 'sex offender' through the recognition of diversity within that category. Attention is also paid to the broader context in which the offender finds him or herself – hence the reference to employment and occupational skills.

The contrasting and sometimes contradictory depictions of the 'teacher' and the 'learner/sex offender' in the above examples illustrates the way in which identity struggles pervade this site, which is further complicated by other stakeholders, particularly psychologists, who have a therapeutic and treatment orientation.

The calculable subject

The institutional *treatment* of the sex offender is arguably dominated by what Rose (1996) refers to as the 'calculable subject', through the administration of a range of standardised psychological tests and other measurements. Table 9.1 lists a panoply of psychological tests in regular use in one centre in Canada. Rose (1996: 120–1) refers to such tests as serving to inscribe the self and its relations:

> diagrams, graphs, tables, charts, numbers – which materializes human qualities in forms amenable to normalisation and calculation. The psychological test rendered visible the invisible qualities of the human soul, distilling the multifarious attributes of the person into a single figure. These inscriptions could be compared one with another, norms could be established, evaluations carried out in relation to those norms and judgements made in the light of these. The psychological test, combining normalization, judgement and truth, becomes a vital procedure . . .

Table 9.1 A list of psychometric tests used with sex offenders in the Regional Treatment Centre, Kingston, Ontario

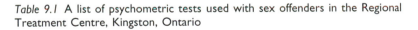

Criminal Sentiments Scale
Balanced Inventory
Cognitive Distortions Child Molester Scale
Miller Intimacy Scale
Buss Durkee Hostility Inventory
Cognitive Distortions Rapists Scale
Empathy Questionnaire
High Risk Situation Test
Muti-phasic Sex Inventory
Adult Self Expression Scale
Michigan Alcohol Screening Test
Relapse Prevention Evaluation Test
Research Questionnaires
Psychological Inventory of Criminal Thinking Styles
Readiness for Treatment Scale

Source: Lundstrom 2002

Thus the tests listed in Table 9.1 are used to make judgements about deviance, appropriate treatment, admission to educational programmes and screening, and progress towards the 'norm' following educational and other interventions. It is common for admission to a programme to be based on the results of such tests and follow-up interviews – those with low literacy levels, low IQ and 'deniers' are frequently prevented from participating. The deployment of these tests allows offenders to be subjected to a normalising and homogenising gaze. For example, they are portrayed as 'lacking' normative qualities such as empathy, the ability to express oneself, the capacity for intimacy, the ability to assert without hostility and so on. Educators are invited to think about learners in these terms which is counter to conventional understandings of learners.

As stated earlier, the educational dimension of programmes for sex offenders is typically conducted in relation to other more psychological interventions. Some typical cognitive behavioural interventions are:

- aversion therapy (the association of inappropriate sexual stimuli with unpleasant sensations);
- orgasmic reconditioning (the substitution of appropriate stimuli for inappropriate stimuli during masturbation);
- satiation (repetition of a fantasy to the point of boredom);
- practising arousal control in everyday situations.

In turn these are supplemented by an armoury of psychopharmacological interventions to manage sexual arousal (anti-androgens such as medroxyprogesterone acetate (Depo-Provera) and mood stabilisers such as fluoxetine (Prozac).

Finally, to the repertoire of interventions can be added an additional measurement 'tool' so to speak – the penile plethysmograph – which is described as

> a physiological tool that measures an offender's sexual arousal pattern or erectile response to certain stimuli. It is typically used in two ways: to measure the offender's sexually deviant interests and ascertain if he has any nondeviant sexual interests ... and as an evaluative tool to measure the success or failure of the behavioral interventions.

> (CSOM 2002: 14)

These physiological and psychological interventions are not themselves examples of what might normally be called pedagogy, but they are carried out in the name of learning (or relearning) and they do contribute to an inscription of the sex offender as a complex of psychological/behavioural attributes: input measures, interventions and output measures all built around changing behaviour. In this regime there is no place for self-understanding, exploration or introspection. Indeed there is no self-work as such, just the measurement and shaping of attitudes and behaviour.

In both the training of sex offender managers (including teachers) and in the treatment of sex offenders the learners are largely invisible in the sense that there is a uniform, homogenous categorisation of the learner as 'sex offender'. No attention is paid to the nature of the sex offence or to the motivation or desires of learners (except in so far as these desires are to be countered). Indeed, there is no sense at all that the learners are engaged in personal change – only that an aspect of their behaviour needs to be expunged.

Disciplinary and professional boundaries

As demonstrated above, a feature of programmes for sex offenders is a multi-team approach, with prison officers, welfare officers, teachers, psychologists, health care workers and others involved in different stages of the programme and in complementary roles. As one teacher respondent remarked:

> Ideally offenders should be contained and the team of carers (lock up staff as well as the teachers, the therapists and the catering staff) that are with them should all have a like minded training so that there is a consistency in the type of response they get from people. Consistency is very important.
>
> (Lundstrom 2002: 24)

Although a seamless team-based approach is desirable, this comment arises partly from the common observation that different professionals worked independently, and with different and often conflicting paradigms. One point of conflict has to do with labelling programmes as 'therapeutic' (the teacher's role being thereby subject to a therapeutic regime) or 'educational'. As a specialist services staff member comments:

'Treatment' of sex offenders implies an illness. If you refer to 'treatment' of sex offenders you collude with a lot of their defence. 'I only did this because I was ill and if you cured me I wouldn't do it again. Therefore I am an ill person, therefore I am not responsible'. Whereas, challenging the behaviour of sex offenders or the re-education of sex offenders is a more appropriate name for the programme. In using 'treatment' the offender can apply a passive approach and say it is the therapist's job to 'cure' him. And if I do re-offend, it is your fault because you did not 'cure' me.

(Lundstrom 2002: 18)

There is evidence that psychologists claim the terrain of therapeutic intervention, which is all very well, but in doing so they see education as restricted to the 'acquisition of knowledge' with the process of personal change being excluded from the role of the educator. The teachers, not surprisingly have different views:

There are different views within education . . . about therapy. One view is that it has nothing to do with education . . . any good educational model addresses the context of people's lives . . . If you are facilitating the development of people who are involved in crime or addictions these are issues which really should come into their learning if possible when people are ready. Particularly if people are in denial and a lot of sex offenders are, you cannot really talk about personal development without addressing those issues.

(Lundstrom 2002: 32)

In the CSOM training material ('Presentation: Methods of Treatment, Section 4) (CSOM 2002: 10–12) there are a number of references to the role of education within an otherwise strongly cognitive behavioural model of treatment:

To modify cognitive distortions and cause an offender to accept responsibility, treatment might include:

- education about denial;
- educating the offender about the relationship of cognitive distortions to sex offender behavior.

To develop victim empathy, treatment might include:

- Psychoeducation on the effects of abuse on victims;
- Teaching empathy skills, such as recognizing emotional distress and communicating empathy.

To control sexual arousal, treatment might include:

- Education about deviant sexual fantasy and its relationship to sexual behavior.

Treatment to improve social competence can include:

- Using the group setting to model, practice and rehearse appropriate and effective social interactions . . . anger management, assertiveness, conflict resolution, leisure time skills, problem solving, stress management, conversational skills, parenting, and substance abuse.

To develop relapse prevention skills, which extend the effects of treatment over time, treatment may include:

- education about relapse prevention as a model for identifying and interrupting the offense cycle;
- teaching strategies to avoid lapses;
- teaching strategies to minimize the extent of lapses.

In the above depiction of educational intervention, education is very much seen as an ancillary part of the treatment regime. As such it is about containing and modifying deviant behaviour, which is certainly not a traditional identity position for a professional educator.

Another significant contestation occurs around the role of prison officers as potential 'facilitators'. On the one hand they are seen to be in close contact with offenders and therefore can offer information and insight into offender behaviours. On the other hand there is a perceived conflict of interest between their disciplinary role and their facilitation role, as an offender respondent explains:

> There could be a conflict of interest for Prison Officers because the role they have to fulfil as part of discipline staff would be at variance with their role as rehabilitation staff. If an offender had a bit of a conflict with a Prison Officer engaged in discipline duties who was also involved in the [sex offender] Programme there might be concerns about confidentiality which could be frightening for offenders.
>
> (Lundstrom 2002: 46)

It is interesting to note that in Lundstrom's study all respondents from the category 'prison management' were positive about the involvement of prison officers as programme facilitators, while all offender and teacher respondents were either ambivalent or against the idea. Specialist services staff, which includes psychologists, were equally divided between positive and 'ambivalent/negative'. A comment from a teacher respondent provides evidence of the professional integrity of teaching being at stake:

> Facilitating a sex offender programme is an area of work where the more skilled and experienced Teachers who have training and education and a lot of further development are reluctant to go. Yet, we are being told staff who do not have that background of training who have all sorts of other barriers arising out of their role as Prison Officers are expected to go in up to their necks. That's crazy!
>
> (Lundstrom 2002: 51)

Professional boundary issues are inevitable in a multi-disciplinary context such as sex offender education, but they are particularly fraught for the teachers in the system, largely because nearly all roles contain an educational dimension, leaving the particular, exclusive role of teachers hard to define and their position marginalised. While psychologists, prison officers, social workers and health workers have narrowly defined tasks within the system which set them aside from other professionals, teachers, or so it seems, have no particular 'markers'. In this context it is interesting, and rather ironic, that 23 per cent of respondents in the survey (prison officers, prison management, specialist services and administration) mentioned that 'Prison Officer Facilitators Sex Offender Programmes should have counselling to alleviate any psychological damage that might be done to them in listening to offenders revealing the extent of their crimes' (Lundstrom 2002: 53). Apparently this is not an issue for teachers!

Concluding comments

This chapter has illustrated the ways in which conventional teacher-learner identities are disrupted by the particular circumstances of sex offender education. It is a site where there are very strong, but nevertheless contested, institutional and community views about the nature of the offender-learners and the purposes of treatment, education and/or punishment. In particular, teacher training materials construct a certain type of teacher and a certain type of learner – but this is contested, both by learners' experiences and teachers' perceptions of their role. For the teachers a great deal of self-work is necessary, in the sense of understanding how one is being positioned by the broader curriculum and the institutional management of sex offenders and how this intersects with previously held perceptions of one's identity as a teacher. The offender-learners are asked to see themselves as a complex of psychological/behavioural attributes; as objects of measurement, evaluation and diagnosis; and as deviant and in need of correction through treatment, education and punishment. They subject themselves, and are subjected to, a behavioural and physiological regime aimed at their 'correction'.

Chapter 10

Pedagogy, identity, reflexivity

The book as a pedagogical practice

In this book we have focused our attention on the relationship between identity and pedagogy in a variety of educational settings. A key position we have taken relates to the plural and changing dimensions of identity as they are manifested in and modified through pedagogical processes. Drawing on our different professional backgrounds and experiences, what we have tried to do is to consider a broad range of pedagogical interventions and discuss them through the common concept of identity. This review has taken us through self-help literature, work-based learning, corporate culture, HIV/AIDS education, gender programmes and sex offender education. In moving through these considerably different settings we have positioned identity and identity change as a common theme through which each can be interrogated. The potential benefits of such a review can be expected to be different for different readers, however from our perspective we have sought to provide a take on pedagogy (*vis-à-vis* identity) that might enable educators to reconsider pedagogy from a potentially novel perspective. This was intended to draw attention to the way that educators are not just narrowly in the business of teaching and learning, but are also involved actively in identity work – work that takes place on both themselves and others. Further, our concern has not been so much with the effectiveness of particular programmes, but rather with constructing a sense of what is going on in the programmes in terms of identity work. Implicit in this approach has been the idea that it is somehow appropriate, beneficial or 'good' for educators to be reflexive about their work in terms of their own and others' identities – indeed with increasing pluralisation of society generally, these issues of being aware of the relations between self and other do seem important.

Thus, we have sought to draw attention to the nature of the identity work that practitioners are involved in. In so doing we have resisted using a formulaic approach where each chapter is written with the same structure and have instead employed different levels of distance from the programmes, different levels of critical engagement and different approaches to understanding learners and those who facilitate learning. Together these case studies did not have as their primary aim an assessment of whether particular pedagogical practices were good or bad, effective or ineffective. Our concern instead was with the identity effects and assumptions that can be inferred from the programmes.

Although we have been explicit throughout the book about discussing identity and pedagogy *per se*, what we have not yet signalled is that this book, and academic texts in general, can be seen as another form of pedagogical practice. This is a pedagogy which proposes that people (i.e. readers) might learn something about practice by reading what others (i.e. writers) have to say about it.

Given that our topic is about identity and pedagogy, we thought it appropriate to close the book with a reflection on our own identity position in relation to the pedagogy of the book. In keeping with the overall ethos of the book, we ask: what are our identities as constructed through this text? What identity positions does our text construct for its readers? What are the pedagogical implications of these identities? And how have we used such identities to create this book? In addressing such questions, we intend that this discussion also be considered as an example of a particular pedagogical practice – the practice of writing books. It is therefore noteworthy that this book is of a particular genre, a genre that could be easily labelled 'academic and theoretical'. Conventionally these types of books are non-fictional, written by people formally associated with universities and make some claim to be presenting new theories and/or new research. In our case this book is also itself an example of a more particular pedagogical practice – it is a book whose topic is explicitly that of pedagogy and learning and it is a book written for a primary audience of fellow academics, students and people interested in pedagogy. The book purports to be able to help its readers learn and come to know something about learning. If we were to follow a simplistic pedagogical logic, we might perhaps propose that the pedagogical process the book involves is one where: 'we write and you read' or 'we write and you learn'. Obviously, this would be a very naive and unreflexive positioning of the book's pedagogy.

In seeking to provide a more reflexive take on our own identities, we connect with a growing concern for attending to reflexivity in academic writing. This concern emerges from a 'reflexive turn' in academic theorising that has resulted from a heightened self-awareness that researchers and theorists play an active role in constructing the 'realities' that they investigate and write about (Chia 1996). Where perhaps there was a traditional view that academic writers were in the business of being objective commentators or analysts of the world around them, there has more recently been a growing critique of the embedded power in the construction of such academic positions. This has, for some, created 'horrid postmodern writing dilemmas' (Richardson 1992: 131) where people who write must do so in the realisation that their writing will inevitably attempt to define and take power over those who are written about and written to. Thus, for Richardson, 'no matter how we stage the text, we – the authors – are doing the staging. As we speak about the people we study, we also speak for them. As we inscribe their lives, we bestow meaning and promulgate values' (p. 131). The call to reflexivity thus suggests that texts might 'interrupt themselves and foreground their own constructedness' (Lather 1991: 124) in an attempt to, at least, acknowledge the power that they try to claim. Thus, reflexivity in writing, and in pedagogical writing in particular, might be written in a way that dispels the conceptualisations of writing that suggest that 'a found world is assumed communicable in a "clear" style in which there is no intrusion by language of an embedded researcher' (Lather 1991: 124). This then suggests that writers (such as ourselves) might adopt a 'reflexive sensitivity and an awareness of the roles occupied by authority and authorship in the production of knowledge [that] invites us to examine our own claims as well as the claims of those we study' (Gubrium and Holstein 1997: 93).

In the same way that teachers may be openly reflexive about their teaching and its pedagogical claims, we too attempt to be openly reflexive about our writing and its pedagogical claims. In a sense we have cordoned off this discussion to this particular part of the book rather than embedding it throughout our text. Our reason is that we did not wish to dwell on our 'selves' throughout the book, and instead do so here both in order to supplement the broader discussion and to discuss reflexivity in identity. In this regard it is worth repeating a small joke told by Marshall Salhins (as reported in Marcus 1994): 'As the Fijian said to the New Ethnographer, "that's enough talking about you; let's talk about me"' (p. 569). This points to the possibility for reflexivity to be textually manifested in extended statements, or even confessions, about a writer's or researcher's own position at the expense of writing about anything else. Thus we believe that 'we need to be careful about forms of textual reflexivity that result in egocentric musings, self-promoting confessionals, and "more reflexive that thou" testimonials' (Rhodes 2000: 522). Although we may be at some risk of such self-centredness we largely limit ourselves to doing so in this particular chapter. Another purpose is to contribute directly to the aims of the book as a whole. For this reason, although we foreground ourselves and 'our' book, we are also commenting on authorial identities more generally.

Author as identity

In terms of the construction of the book, we are five academics who are writing a single book from the textual position of a common 'we' – five individual identities coalesced into one for the purpose of generating a position from which to write. Thus, we have tried, in assembling this text, to create a new identity from which to narrate. This perhaps infers (quite falsely) that we are all writing this book as if we together were reciting these words in a harmonious chorus. Of course this is not the case. By even the most conventional categorisations (gender, age, cultural background etc.) we are quite different. Further, we have vastly different experiences and backgrounds in pedagogy and on many topics we disagree with one another. In some ways it is on the basis of our differences (in terms of research interests, professional experiences etc.) that we have been able to produce a book that interrogates such a broad range of pedagogical practices. These differences are also important because we have had to work to actively manage them in terms of how we can write from a common position. To some degree academic identities are defined by particular research interests and the theoretical positions that one brings to them. Thus, for each of us, to be associated individually as the authors of texts which, in part, have been written by others means that we have had to assess whether these other texts are conceivable within our own self-defined (or self-desired) identity positions. Such a questioning led us into debates, contestations and compromises over what should or should not be included in the book and what type of theories we should draw on or try to develop. The 'we' of the book has been forged out of contestation and debate through which we had to be prepared to associate each individual 'I' with our collective 'we'. Thus, inside the text, we are homogenised into a single 'we'.

To the extent that this book has a narrative element to it, this narrative constructs the collective identity that we have tried to negotiate for ourselves. Importantly, it does so by positioning us not necessarily as 'characters' in the narrative, but as its narrators. The book has an 'effect of signature' (Derrida 1982: 328) such that the inclusion of our proper names on the front cover as the authors of the book confers on us the authority of being the book's narrators. Thus our identity is constructed as being both authoritative and homogeneous. This in turn forms identity positions which attempt to confer on us power in the pedagogical practice of the book – it tries to set us up as the 'knowers' in agreement. This is not solely of our own doing; the existence of the genre of this book both as a text and as a narrative pre-exists our writing of the book – the identity position of the author is available to us through pre-existing narratives which are drawn on in attempting to fashion us as author(itie)s. We write these narratives about learning and so forth in a way that positions them as putative representations of our experience, thoughts and ideas, but in order to do so we draw on pre-existing narratives that include the characterisation of authorial identity (what we referred to in Chapter 3 as 'relational narratives'). Thus, more generally, our act of writing is an act of identity which aligns us to pre-existing and socio-culturally shaped subject positions which work to reproduce dominant beliefs, interests and values (Ivanic 1998).

The character of such authorial identity positions, as they are socially defined, is particularly evident as one reads the texts that accompany books. Usually appearing on the back or inside covers, these texts include biographical comments on the author(s), summaries of the book's content and quotations by others on the book. To use a well known example, if one takes a book like Michel Foucault's (1986) *The Care of the Self*[1], one finds out that 'Michel Foucault was one of the most influential thinkers in the contemporary world' (inside cover), that Roy Porter from the London Review of Books thinks that the book is a 'remarkable achievement', that Foucault is 'a superb practitioner of conventional intellectual history' (back cover), and that the book contains a 'graphic and perceptive depiction of [how the] crucial shift in sexual attitudes deepens our understanding of the modern experience of sexuality' (back cover). These quotations reflect common cultural definitions of authorial identity. Their purpose is to construct the author as a powerful agent of knowledge and truth and to imply that by reading his or her works the reader might also be able to share in this knowledge. The narrative that positions the author as the supreme knower is a common one with which academic writers must deal. In our own case we must also deal with such authorial identitiy positions in our writing (just as teachers need to deal with narratives that position them as knowers). We know, for example, that in the context of our professional careers as academics it is of value to be able to write oneself into an authorial narrative – one where the writing and publishing of books and other works is a way of becoming a particular kind of (non-teaching) academic. This, in turn, is related to other very powerful considerations such as reputation, promotability and standing within academic communities. Thus in writing this book we are also writing ourselves as particular types of academics.

If we move on from how our identities can be textually manufactured as authors, it is not difficult to see that the other identity practices we refer to throughout the book (teachers, students, workers etc.) are identities which we, from time to time, do draw (and have drawn) on to define ourselves. All of us have been students. All of us have been academic teachers. All of us have been workers of different types. So we are using one mode of identity that we occupy (the author) to write about other modes of identity that we also do and have occupied. However, we highlight and privilege our authorial identities. This is such that our identities become fragmented as we momentarily privilege our author identities to construct ourselves as 'knowers' who are somehow able to collectively comment from afar on the everyday practices that we write about. In this context, however, other aspects of our identities are sidelined as the narratives we write position us primarily as author identities. Hence we write ourselves in as authors by drawing on pre-existing categories of persons that 'exist'. In so doing, we inevitably attempt to place ourselves in a position of relative power. We are five people with many identities, but only one emerges here as being dominant.

Authors and subjects

Despite the unifying identity of the 'we' from which this book is written, the actual writing of the book, like many co-authored books, was not a process where we all wrote everything. Such an approach would be untenable and mechanically impossible. Instead, each of us has taken the lead in writing different chapters – so there is an 'I' who is writing these very words you read, yet they are written from a 'we' perspective. Indeed, for some chapters of the book, some of us have made little or no contribution and for others we have been very primary in the writing. Some of us might disagree with or dislike what was included in a chapter that was not written by us. We will save you from the details of such possible conflicts, however the point is that these differences are largely swept aside because we are all together in the name of a single identity – the authorial 'we'.

Of course our identity as authors is such that the concept of author does not 'refer simply and purely to a real individual' (Foucault 1984: 113). Instead, our positions within the pedagogical practice of this book create us as authors. Our identity as authors is produced by this text rather than the text being produced by the authors. So, it is worth noting that the narrative of this text is such that it (re)constructs a number of identity positions to which people might relate – author, learner, student, teacher, worker etc. In confirming these possible identities, we take on the identity of the author of the text. You can read this text and you might be able to 'identify' with one or more of these different identities and use them to characterise yourself – either in terms of identifying with them or seeing yourself other to them. Further, in writing about these characterised identities, we did not create them from 'thin air' – they were available to use culturally through other narratives in which we have been involved. Thus pedagogically this text creates different identities based on pre-existing categorisations of social identity and uses them to tell its story. Further, in telling this story there is an identity politics at work – one that attempts to place the identity of its authors as being in a position of power where we 'know', and try (inevitably failing) to position the readers as the recipients of this knowledge. Invariably this is one of the many forms of power at work in a variety of pedagogical sites, one where she or he who teaches works with power over he or she who learns.

Despite our active involvement in this book our status as authors is socially defined rather than being controlled by us. The modern figure of the author on which we draw to define ourselves is one that posits the author as being the originator of a text; a text which, at an extreme, is deemed to be the 'message' of the 'Author-God' (Barthes 1977: 146) who confides in her or his readers secrets and ultimate meanings that might otherwise be unavailable to them. Practically, however, this is clearly not the case, although modern notions of the author still enable people who write to use their writing to attempt to assign themselves privileged forms of identity as knowers and revealers. As Barthes argues, however, the author as a person does not need to be regarded as the originator of the text – indeed it would seem that the opposite is true. That is to say, the book precedes the author rather than the author preceding the book. Language is performative and in this case it performs our identities as authors. Acknowledging this, however, does not make the author-as-knower narrative any less powerful – theoretically contested perhaps, but still culturally potent. The act of having written a book of a particular type is a way that people such as us can lay a claim to authority whereas prior to the writing our potential authority may have been less. We are not authors who write, but rather writers who inadvertently aspire to be authors by virtue of the academic genre in which we choose to write. Of course, our reflexive comment here is an attempt to trouble this authoritisation, but not one that eradicates it. As Barthes put it: 'no writer who began in a lonely struggle against the power of language could or can avoid being coopted by it' (Barthes 1977/1993: 467).

This process of the generation of authors is active in the writing of this book and in academic writing more generally – it is an effect of the genre in which we write such that the power of writing is not one attempted by an 'author as person' but rather is brought forth through the established tenets of the genre (Rhodes 2002). Here there is a complex relationship between producing knowledge through writing and the production of the subjectivity of a particular type of knower/ writer such that to become an academic writer one must learn to reproduce particular writing conventions (Lee 1998) and in so doing become co-opted into particular forms of identity. Within such a process, however, not everyone has the potential or desire to write themselves into such privileged forms of identity. Further, this inabil-ity or unwillingness to do so has material effects in other ways – indeed, historically, most books were written by educated white men. So, on the one hand 'textual collusion' is problematic in the sense that it is the 'enactment of pedagogies, the (re)production of curric-ular knowledge and the formation of subjects' (Fuller and Lee 1997: 410). On the other hand, this is also problematic because some people might be excluded from even attempting such forms of collusion.

Concluding comments

In the light of the problematics of our identity and authority, our intentions are not just expressive or reflexive but also communicative. Concurrently we realise that despite our ability to consider the iden-tity effects of our writing, such effects are not solely determined by us. Thus we have written a book that we hope people will read and connect with. We have tried to influence the nature of these potential connections but, of course, how they are played out is guided as much by your reading as it is by our writing. It is our hope that in reading the book you have been able to make some productive connections that have resulted in some 'lines of flight' (Deleuze and Guattari 1987) for your own thinking and practice. This does not mean, necessarily, agreeing or disagreeing with us, but rather that the text may have had some pragmatic use for a creative encounter with possible ways of understanding and doing practice. Unavoidably yet willingly we leave it with you to decide if, or to what extent, this is the case.

Note

1 We are referring here to the Penguin paperback edition printed in 1990.

References

Alvesson, M. and Berg, P-O. (1992) *Corporate Culture and Organizational Symbolism*. Berlin: de Gruyter.

Alvesson, M. and Willmott, H. (2002) 'Identity Regulation as Organizational Control: Producing the Appropriate Individual', *Journal of Management Studies*, 39(5): 619–44.

Anderson, G., Boud, D., Cohen, R. and Sampson, J. (1998) 'Students Guide to Learning Partnerships', in *Peer Learning: A Guide for Staff and Students*. Sydney: University of Sydney Technology.

Anderson, H. and Goolishian, H. (1992) 'The Client is the Expert: A Not Knowing Approach to Therapy', in S. McNamee and K. Gergen (eds) *Therapy as Social Construction*. London: Sage.

Aronowitz, S. (1994) *Dead Artists, Live Theories and Other Cultural Problems*. New York: Routledge.

Australia DEET (Department of Education, Employment and Training) (undated) *Gender Inclusive Teaching in TAFE*. Canberra: DEET.

Bakhtin, M.M. (1981) *The Dialogic Imagination: Four Essays*, trans. C. Emerson and M. Holquist, ed. M. Holquist. Austin, TX: University of Texas Press.

Baudrillard, J. (1989) *America*. London: Verso.

Bauman, Z. (1996) 'From Pilgrim to Tourist – Or a Short History of Identity', in S. Hall and P. du Gay (eds) *Questions of Cultural Identity*. London: Sage.

Barthes, R. (1977) *Image, Music, Text*. London: Fontana.

Barthes, R. (1977/1993) 'Authors and Writers', in S. Sontag (ed.) *A Roland Barthes Reader*, pp. 185–93. London: Blackwell.

Beck, U. (1992) *Risk Society: Towards a New Modernity*. London: Sage.

Beck, U., Giddens, A., and Lash, S. (1994) *Reflexive Modernization: Politics, Tradition and Aesthetics in the Modern Social Order*. Cambridge: Polity Press.

Bernstein, B.B. (1996) *Pedagogy, Symbolic Control and Identity: Theory, Research, Critique*. London: Taylor & Francis.

Bhaba, H.K. (1992) 'Postcolonial Authority and Postmodern Guilt', in L. Grossberg, C. Nelson and P. Treichler (eds) *Cultural Studies*. New York: Routledge.

Bhabha, H.K. (1996) 'Unpacking my Library . . . Again', in I. Chambers and L. Curti (eds) *The Post-colonial Question: Common Skies Divided Horizons*. London: Routledge.

Binney, G. and Williams, C. (1997) *Learning into the Future: Changing the Way People Change Organizations*. London: Nicholas Brealey Publishing.

Binswanger, L. (1958) 'The Case of Ellen West: An Anthropological-Clinical Study', in R. May, E. Angel and H.F. Ellenberger (eds) *Existence: A New Dimension in Psychiatry and Psychology*, pp. 237–364. New York: Basic Books.

Birke, L. and Silvertown, J. (1984) *More than the Parts: Biology and Politics*. London: Pluto Press.

Blake, T. (2000) *Planning and Review Unit UTS Public Documents*. Sydney: University of Technology Sydney.

Boud, D. (1989) 'Some Competing Traditions in Experiential Learning', in S. Weil and I. McGill (eds) *Making Sense of Experiential Learning*. Milton Keynes: Open University Press.

Boud, D. and Solomon, N. (2001a) 'Repositioning Universities and Work', in D. Boud and N. Solomon (eds) *Work-based Learning: A New Higher Education?* Buckingham: Open University Press.

Boud, D. and Solomon, N. (eds) (2001b) *Work-based learning: A New Higher Education?* Buckingham: Open University Press.

Boud, D., Keogh, R. and Walker, D. (1985) *Reflection: Turning Experience Into Learning*. London: Kogan Page.

Bradbury, M. and McFarlane, M. (eds) (1976) *Modernism*. London: Penguin.

Brookfield, S. (1991) 'Using Critical Incidents to Explore Assumptions', in J. Mezirow *et al.* (eds) *Fostering Critical Reflection in Adulthood*. San Francisco, CA: Jossey-Bass.

Brookfield, S. (1995) *Becoming a Critically Reflective Teacher*. San Francisco, CA: Jossey-Bass.

Burbules, N.C. (1995) 'Postmodern Doubt in the Philosophy of Education', paper presented to the 'Philosophy of Education Annual Conference', San Francisco, 29 March–3 April.

Butler, J. (1993) *Bodies that Matter*. London: Routledge.

Butler-Bowden, T. (2001) *50 Self-help Classics*. Sydney: Simon & Schuster.

Byrne, J.A. (2002) 'Inside McKinsey', *Business Week*. 8 July: 66–76.

Carnegie, D. (1999) *How to Win Friends and Influence People*. Sydney: HarperCollins.

Casey, C. (1995) *Work, Self and Society: After Industrialism*. London: Routledge.

Casey, C. (1999) ' "Come, Join Our Family": Discipline and Integration in Corporate Organizational Culture', *Human Relations*, 52(2): 155–78.

Castel, R. (1991) 'From Dangerousness to Risk', in G. Burchell, C. Gordon and P. Miller (eds) *The Foucault Effect: Studies in Governmentality*. London: Harvester Wheatsheaf.

Cave, M. (2002) 'Go Ahead, Motivate Me!', *Australian Financial Review*, 14 June: 30.

Chan, A. (2000) *Critically Constituting Organization*. Amsterdam: John Benjamins.

Chappell, C., Farrell, L., Scheeres, H. and Solomon, N. (2000) 'The Organization of Identity: Four Cases', in C. Symes and J. McIntyre (eds) *Working Knowledge: The New Vocationalism and Higher Education*, pp. 135–52, Buckingham: Open University Press.

Chia, R. (1996) *Organizational Analysis as Deconstructive Practice*. Berlin: de Gruyter.

Chopra, D. (1996) *The Seven Spiritual Laws of Success: A Practical Guide to the Fulfilment of your Dreams*. London: Bantam.

Coats, M. (1996) *Recognizing Good Practice in Women's Education and Training*. Leicester: National Institute of Adult Continuing Education.

Collins, D. (1995) *Organizational Change: Sociological Perspectives*. London: Sage.

Covey, S. (1990) *The 7 Habits of Highly Effective People*. New York: Simon and Schuster.

Crawford, J., Baxter, D., Cooper, D., de Ven, P.V., Noble, J., Kippax, S. and Prestage, G. (1997) 'Gay Youth and their Precautionary Sexual Behaviours: The Sydney Men and Sexual Health Study', *AIDS Education and Prevention*, 9(5): 395–410.

CSOM (Center for Sex Offender Management) (2002) *Supervision of Sex Offenders in the Community: A Training Curriculum Prepared for the Office of Justice Programs, U.S. Department of Justice by the Center for Sex Offender Management*. www.csom.org/train/supervision/index.html, accessed 15 August 2002.

Culley, M. (1985) 'Anger and Authority in the Introductory Women's Studies Classroom', in M. Culley and C. Portuges (eds) *Gendered Subjects: The Dynamics of Feminist Teaching*, pp. 209–18. Boston, MA: Routledge.

Culley, M., Diamond, A., Edwards, L., Lennox, S. and Portuges, C. (1985) 'The Politics of Nurturance', in M. Culley and C. Portuges (eds) *Gendered Subjects: The Dynamics of Feminist Teaching*, pp, 11–20. Boston, MA: Routledge.

Dahler-Larsen, P. (1994) 'Corporate Culture and Morality: Durkheim-Inspired Reflections on the Limits of Corporate Culture', *Journal of Management Studies*, 31(1): 1–18.

de Peuter, J. (1998) 'The Dialogues of Narrative Identity', in M.M. Bell and M. Gardiner (eds) *Bakhtin and the Human Sciences: No Last Word*, pp. 30–48. London: Sage.

Deal, T. and Kennedy, A. (1999) *The New Corporate Cultures*. London: Texere.

Dean, M. and Hindess, B. (eds) (1998) *Governing Australia: Studies in Contemporary Rationalities of Government*. Cambridge: Cambridge University Press.

Deleuze, G. (1983) *Nietzsche and Philosophy*, trans. H. Tomlinson. New York: Columbia University Press.

Deleuze, G. and Guattari, F. (1987) *A Thousand Plateaus: Capitalism and Schizophrenia*, trans. B. Massumi. Minneapolis, MN: University of Minnesota Press.

Denton, J. (1998) *Organizational Learning and Effectiveness*. London: Routledge.

Derrida, J. (1978) *Writing and Difference*. London: Routledge & Kegan Paul.

Derrida, J. (1982) *Margins of Philosophy*. Chicago, IL: University of Chicago Press.

Detert, J.R., Schroeder, R.G. and Mauriel, J.J. (2000) 'A Framework for Aligning Culture and Improvement Initiatives in Organizations', *Academy of Management Review*, 25(4): 850–63.

Dryfoos (1991) 'Preventing High Risk Behavior', *American Journal of Public Health*, 81: 157–8.

du Gay, P. (1996a) *Consumption and Identity at Work*. London: Sage.

du Gay, P. (1996b) 'Organizing Identity: Entrepreneurial Governance and Public Management', in S. Hall and P. du Gay (eds) *Questions of Cultural Identity*, pp. 151–69. London: Sage.

Edwards, R., Ranson, S. and Strain, M. (2002) Reflexivity: Towards a Theory of Lifelong Learning', *International Journal of Lifelong Education*, 21(6): 525–36.

Elliot, A. (1996) *Subject to Ourselves: Social Theory, Psycho-analysis and Postmodernity*. Cambridge: Polity Press.

Ellsworth, E. (1989) 'Why Doesn't This Feel Empowering? Working Through the Repressive Myths of Critical Pedagogy', *Harvard Educational Review*, 59(3): 297–324.

Eraut, M. (2000) Non-formal Learning, Implicit Learning and Tacit Knowledge in Professional Work', in F. Coffield (ed.) *The Necessity of Informal Learning*, pp. 377–406. Bristol: The Policy Press.

Erikson, E. (1977) *Childood and Society*. London: Methuen.

Ewald, F. (1991) 'Insurance and Risk', in G. Burchell, C. Gordon and P. Miller (eds) *The Foucault Effect: Studies in Governmentality*. London: Harvester Wheatsheaf.

Feasey, A. (2002) 'What Business are Businesses Really In?' *Business Spirit Journal Online*, www.bizspirit.com/bsj/archives/bsjarchive/fasey.htm, accessed 12 August 2002.

Field, L. (2001) *Self-esteem Workbook: An Interactive Approach to Changing Your Life*. London: Random House.

Foucault, M. (1977) *The Archeology of Knowledge*, trans. A.M. Sheridan Smith. London: Tavistock.

Foucault, M. (1980) *Power/Knowledge: Selected Interviews and Other Writings 1972–1977*, trans. C. Gordon, L. Marshall, J. Mepham and K. Soper, ed. C. Gordon. New York: Pantheon.

Foucault, M. (1983) 'The Subject and Power', in H. Dreyfus, and P. Rabinow (eds) *Michel Foucault: Beyond Structuralism and Hermeneutics*, pp. 208–26. Chicago, IL: University of Chicago Press.

Foucault, M. (1984) 'What is an Author?', in P. Rabinow (ed.) *The Foucault Reader*, pp. 101–20. Harmondsworth: Penguin.

Foucault, M. (1986) *The Care of the Self, The History of Sexuality*, vol. 3, trans. R. Hurley. Harmondsworth: Penguin.

Foucault (1988) 'Technologies of the Self', in L. Martin, H. Gutman and P. Hutton (eds) *Technologies of the Self: A Seminar with Michel Foucault*, pp. 16–49. Amherst, MA: University of Massachusetts Press.

Foucault, M. (1991) 'Governmentality', in G. Burchell, C. Gordon and P. Miller (eds) *The Foucault Effect, Studies in Governmentality*, pp. 53–72. Chicago, IL: The University of Chicago Press.

Fox, C. and Trinca, H. (2001) 'The Big Idea', *The Australian Financial Review*, 13 July.

Freire, P. (1972) *Pedagogy of the Oppressed*. Harmondsworth: Penguin.

Freire, P. (1973) *Education for Critical Consciousness*. New York: Herter & Herter.

Fuller, G. and Lee, A. (1997) 'Textual Collusions', *Discourse: Studies in the Cultural Politics of Education*, 18(3): 409–15.

Furlong, A. and Cartmel, F. (1997) *Young People and Social Change*. Buckingham: Open University Press.

Garrick, J. and Solomon, N. (2001) 'Technologies of Learning at Work: Disciplining the Self', in V. Sheared and P.A. Sissel (eds) *Making Space: Merging Theory and Practice in Adult Education*, pp. 301–13, Westport, CT: Bergin & Garvey.

Gee, J.G. (2000) 'The New Capitalism: What's New?', *Working Knowledge Conference Proceedings*, pp. 89–194. Sydney: University of Technology Sydney.

Gee, J.G., Hull, G. and Lankshear, C. (1996) *The New Work Order: Behind the Language of the New Capitalism*. St Leonards: Allen & Unwin.

Geiger, B. and Tierney, M. (1996) 'My Guardian Angel: A Learning Exercise for Adolescent AIDS Education, *AIDS Education and Prevention*, 8(1): 86–91.

Gergen, K.J. and Gergen, M.M. (1988) 'Narrative and the Self as Relationship', in L. Berkowitz (ed.) *Advances in Experimental Psychology*, pp. 17–56. New York: Academic Press.

Gergen, K.J. and Kaye, J. (1992) 'Beyond Narrative in the Negotiation of Therapeutic Meaning', in S. McNamee and K.J. Gergen (eds) *Therapy as Social Construction*, pp. 166–85. London: Sage.

Giddens, A. (1991) *Modernity and Self-Identity*. Cambridge: Polity Press.

Giddens, A. (ed.) (1994) *The Polity Reader in Gender Studies*. Cambridge: Polity Press.

Giroux, H.A. (1998) 'Teenage Sexuality', in J.S. Epstein (ed.) *Youth Culture Identity in a Postmodern World*. Oxford: Blackwell.

Gleick, J. (1988) *Chaos Making a New Science*. London: Heinemann.

Goleman, D. (1996) *Emotional Intelligence*. London: Bloomsbury.

Gordon, C. (1991) 'Governmental Rationality: An Introduction', in G. Burchell, C. Gordon and P. Miller (eds) *The Foucault Effect, Studies in Governmentality*, pp. 1–52. Chicago, IL: The University Chicago Press.

Greenblatt, M. and Robinson, M. (1993) 'Life Styles, Adaptive Starategies and Sexual Behaviour of Homeless Adolescents, *Hospital and Community Psychiatry*, 44: 1177–89.

Grosz, E.A. (1989) *Sexual Subversions: Three French Feminists*. Sydney: Allen & Unwin.

Gubrium, J.F. and Holstein, J.A. (1997) *The New Language of Qualitative Method*. New York: Oxford University Press.

Habermas, J. (1985) *The Philosophical Discourse of Modernity*. Cambridge: Polity Press.

Hall, S. (1996) 'Introduction: Who Needs Identity?' in S. Hall and P. du Gay (eds) *Questions of Cultural Identity*, pp. 1–17. London: Sage.

Hall, S. and du Gay, P. (eds) (1996) *Questions of Cultural Identity*. London: Sage.

Hall, S. and Jacques, M. (1989) *New Times: The Changing Face of Politics in the 1990s*. London: Lawrence & Wisehart.

Hansen, L. (2000) 'Semi-skilled, Mature Men in Adult Education – Motivation and Barriers, *Working Knowledge Conference Proceedings*, pp. 573–8. Sydney: University of Technology Sydney.

Hardt, M. and Negri, A. (2001) *Empire*. Cambridge, MA: Harvard University Press.

Harris, L.C. and Ogbona, E. (2002) 'The Unintended Consequences of Culture Interventions: A Study of Unexpected Outcomes,' *British Journal of Management*, 13: 31–49.

Hart, M.U. (1990) 'Liberation Through Consciousness Raising', in J. Mezirow (ed.) *Fostering Critical Reflection in Adulthood*. San Francisco, CA: Jossey-Bass.

Harvey, D. (1990) *The Condition of Postmodernity: An Enquiry into the Origins of Cultural Change*. Oxford: Blackwell.

Hatton, N. and Smith, D. (1995) 'Reflection in Teacher Education: Towards Definition and Implementation', *Teaching and Teacher Education*, 11(1): 33–49.

Hay, L. (1987) *You Can Heal Your Life*. Sydney: Hay House.

Hazen, M.A. (1993) 'Towards Polyphonic Organisation', *Journal of Organizational Change Management*, 6(5): 15–26.

Hekman, S. (1994) 'The Feminist Critique of Rationality', in A. Giddens (ed.) *The Polity Reader in Gender Studies*, pp. 50–61. Cambridge: Polity Press.

Henriques, J., Holloway, W., Urwin, C., Venn, C. and Walkerdine, V. (1994) *Changing the Subject: Psychology, Social Regulation and Subjectivity*. London: Methuen.

hooks b. (1990) *Yearning: Race, Gender and Cultural Politics*. Boston, MA: South End Press.

Humphries, S. (1991) *The Secret World of Sex*. London: Sidgwick & Jackson.

Hutner, J. (2002) 'Evolutionary Business', *Business Spirit Journal Online*, http://bizspirit.com/bsj/archives/bsjarchive/hutner1.htm, accessed 12 August 2002.

Ibarra-Colado, E. (2002) 'Organizational Paradoxes and Business Ethics: In Search of New Modes of Existence', in S. Clegg (ed.) *Management and Organization Paradoxes*, pp. 165–84. Amsterdam: John Benjamins.

Ivanic, R. (1998) *Writing and Identity: The Discoursal Construction of Identity in Academic Writing*. Amsterdam: John Benjamins.

Jantz, N. and Becker, M.H. (1984) 'The Health Belief Model: A Decade Later, *Health Education Quarterly*, 11: 1–47.

Johnson, T.P., Aschkenasy, J.R., Herbers, M.R. and Gillenwater, T. (1996) 'Self-reported Risk Factors for AIDS Among Homeless Youth', *AIDS Education and Prevention*, 8(4): 308–22.

Kelly, G. (ed.) (1989) *International Handbook of Women's Education*. New York: Greenwood Press.

Kemmis, S. and McTaggart, R. (1988) *The Action Research Planner*. Victoria: Deakin University.

Kirby, D., Korpi, M., Adivi, C. and Weissman, J. (1997) 'An Impact Evaluation of Project SNAPP: An AIDS and Pregnancy Prevention Middle School Program, *AIDS Education and Prevention*, 9: 44–61.

Kohn, R. (2000) 'The New Business Prophets', *Radio National Online*, http://www.abc.net.au/rn/relig/spirit/stories/s222069.htm, accessed 19 July 2002.

Lacan, J. (1968) *The Language of the Self: The Function of Language in Psychoanalysis*. Baltimore, MD: Johns Hopkins University Press.

Landmark Education (2001) *Curriculum for Living*, Part 1. San Francisco: Landmark Education Forum.

Lather, P. (1991) *Getting Smart: Feminist Research and Pedagogy With/in the Postmodern*. London: Routledge.

LEBD (Landmark Education Business Development) (2002) www.lebd.com, accessed 21 August 2002.

Lee, A. (1998) 'Doctoral Research as Writing', in J. Higgs (ed.) *Writing Qualitative Research*, pp. 124–42. Sydney: Hampden Press.

Lesko, N. (1996) 'Past, Present and Future Conceptions of Adolescence', *Educational Theory*, 46: 453–72.

Lewis, M. and Simon, R. (1986) 'A Discourse Not Intended for Her: Learning and Teaching Within Patriarchy', *Harvard Educational Review*, 56(4): 457–72.

Lloyd, G. (1984) *The Man of Reason: 'Male' and 'Female' in Western Philosophy*. London: Methuen.

Locke, J. ([1690] 1959) *An Essay Concerning Human Understanding*. New York: Dover Publications.

Logan, D.C. (1998) *Transforming the Network of Conversations in BHP New Zealand Steel: Landmark Education Business Development's New Paradigm for Organizational Change*, Case 1984–01. Los Angles, CA: Marshall School of Business, University of Southern California.

Luke, C. and Gore, J. (1992) (eds) *Feminisms and Critical Pedagogy*. New York: Routledge.

Lundstrom, F. (2002) *The Development of a New Multi-Disciplinary Sex Offender Rehabilitation Programme for the Irish Prison Service*. Dublin: Government Publications.

Lyotard, J-F. (1984) *The Postmodern Condition: A Report on Knowledge*. Minneapolis, MN: University of Minnesota Press.

Lyotard, J-F. (1992) *The Postmodern Explained to Children: Correspondence 1982–1985*. Sydney: Power Publications.

Marchetti, M. (1999) 'Soul Searching', *Sales and Marketing Management*, October: 47–60.

Marcus, G.E. (1994) 'What Comes (Just) After "Post"? The Case of Ethnography', in N.K. Denzin and Y.S. Lincoln (eds) *Handbook of Qualitative Research*, pp. 563–74. Thousand Oaks, CA: Sage.

Marzano, R.J., Zaffron, S., Zraik, L., Robbins, S.L. and Yoon, L. (1995) 'A New Paradigm for Educational Change', *Education*, 116(2): 162–73.

McCarl, S.R., Zaffron, S., McCarl Nielson, J. and Kennedy, S.L. (2001) 'The Promise of Philosophy and the Landmark Forum', *Contemporary Philosophy*, 13(1/2): 51–9.

McIntyre, J. and Solomon, N. (2000) 'The Policy Environment of Work-based Learning: Globalization, Institutions and Workplaces', in C. Symes and J. McIntyre (eds) *Working Knowledge: The New Vocationalism and Higher Education*. Buckingham: Open University Press.

McIntyre, J., Chappell, C., Scheeres, H., Solomon, N., Symes, C. and Tennant, M. (1999) *The RAVL Symposium: New Questions about Work and Learning, Working Paper, 99.22*. Research Centre for Vocational Education and Training (RCVET). Sydney: UTS.

McKenna, K. (1997) 'Working with Difference Differently: Exploring the Subtext of Pedagogical Interactions', *Curriculum Studies*, 5(1): 49–68.

McLeod, J. (2000) 'Schooling and Subjectivity in a Longitudinal Study of Secondary Students', *British Journal of Sociology of Education*, 21(4): 501–21.

McLeod, J. (2001) 'Metaphors of the Self: Searching for Young People's Identity Through Inteviews', in J.M.K. Malone (ed.) *Researching Youth*. Hobart: National Clearinghouse for Youth Studies.

McLeod, J., Yates, L. and Halasa, K. (1994) 'Voice, Difference and Feminist Pedagogy', *Curriculum Studies*, 2(2): 189–202.

Mezirow, J. (1990) *Fostering Critical Reflection in Adulthood: A Guide to Transformative and Emancipatory Learning*. San Francisco, CA: Jossey-Bass.

Mezirow, J. (1991) *Transformative Dimensions of Adult Learning*. San Francisco, CA: Jossey-Bass.

Miller, J. (1993) *The Passion of Michel Foucault*. London: HarperCollins.

Miller, P. and Rose, N. (1990) 'Governing Economic Life', *Economy and Society*, 19: 1–31.

Miller, P. and Rose, N. (1993) 'Governing Economic Life', in M. Gane and T. Johnson (eds) *Foucault's New Domains*, pp. 75–105. London: Routledge.

Misko, J. (1999) *Transition Pathways: What Happens to Young People When They Leave School*. Leabrook, S. Australia: NCVER.

OECD (Organisation for Economic Cooperation and Development) (1999) *Preparing Youth for the 21st Century: The Transition from Education to the Labour Market: Proceedings of the Washington D.C. Conference, 23–24 February*. Paris: OECD.

Parker, M. (2000) *Organizational Culture and Identity: Unity and Division at Work*. London: Sage.

Pateman, C. (1989) *The Disorder of Women*. Cambridge: Polity Press.

Perryman, M. (ed.) (1994) *Altered States: Postmodernism Politics Culture*. London: Lawrence & Wisehart.

Peters, T.J. and Waterman, R.H. (1982) *In Search of Excellence: Lessons From America's Best Run Companies*, New York: Harper & Row.

Pheasant, B. (2001) Business Searches for a Soul, *Australian Financial Review*, 21 April.

Polk, K. (1993) 'Reflections on Youth Subcultures', in R. White (ed.) *Youth Subcultures: Theory, History and the Australian Experience*. Hobart: National Clearinghouse for Youth Studies.

Reed, M. (1998) 'Organizational Analysis as Discourse Analysis: A Critique', in D. Grant, T. Keenoy and C. Oswick (eds) *Discourse and Organization*, pp. 193–212. London: Sage.

Rennie, M. and Bellin, M. (1999) 'Raising the Consciousness and Profits of Business', paper presented at the International Conference on Business and Consciousness, Acapulco, 6–12 November.

Rhodes, C. (2000) ' "Doing" Knowledge At Work: Dialogue, Monologue and Power in Organizational Learning', in J. Garrick and C. Rhodes (eds) *Research and Knowledge at Work: Perspectives, Case-studies and Innovative Strategies*. London: Routledge.

Rhodes, C. (2001) *Writing Organization: (Re)presentation and Control in Narratives at Work*, Amsterdam: John Benjamins.

Rhodes, C. (2002) 'Text, Plurality and Organizational Knowledge/I Like to Write About Organizations', *Ephemera: Critical Dialogues on Organization*, 2(2): 98–118.

Rhodes, C. and Garrick, J. (2000) 'Inside the Knowledge Works: Reviewing the Terrain', in J. Garrick and C. Rhodes (eds) *Research and Knowledge at Work: Perspectives, Case-studies and Innovative Strategies*, pp. 271–7. London: Routledge.

Rhodes, C. and Garrick, J. (2002) 'Economic Metaphors and Working Knowledge: Enter the "Cogito-Economic" Subject', *Human Resources Development International*, 5(1): 87–97.

Richardson, L.L. (1992) 'Writing: A Method of Inquiry', in N.K. Denzin and Y.S. Lincoln (eds) *Handbook of Qualitative Research*, pp. 516–29. Thousand Oaks, CA: Sage.

Richardson, C. (2001) *Life Makeovers: 52 Practical and Inspiring Ways to Improve Your Life One Week at a Time*. London: Bantam.

Ricoeur, P. (1992) *Oneself as Another*, trans. K. Blamey. Chicago, IL: University of Chicago Press.

Robbins, A. (1992) *Awaken the Giant Within: How to Take Immediate Control of Your Mental, Emotional, Physical and Financial Destiny*. New York: Simon & Schuster.

Rogers, C.R. (1983) *Freedom to Learn for the 1980s*. Columbus, OH: Merrill.

Rogers, R.W. (1984) 'Changing Health Related Attitudes and Behaviour: The Role of Preventative Health Psychology', in J. Harvey, J.E. Maddux, R.P. McGlynn, P.H. Rossi and H. Freeman (eds) *Evaluation: A Systematic Approach*. London: Sage.

Rorty, R. (1989) *Contingency Irony and Solidarity*. Cambridge: Cambridge University Press.

Rosaldo, R. (1993) *Culture and Truth*. London: Routledge.

Rose, N. (1996) *Inventing Our Selves: Psychology, Power and Personhood*. Cambridge: Cambridge University Press.

Rose, N. (1999) *Powers of Freedom: Reframing Political Thought*. Cambridge: Cambridge University Press.

Rossiter, A. (1997) 'Putting Order in its Place: Disciplining Pedagogy', *Curriculum Studies*, 5(1): 29–38.

Scheeres, H. and Solomon, N. (2000) 'Research Partnerships at Work: New Identities for New Times', in J. Garrick and C. Rhodes (eds) *Research and*

Knowledge at Work: Perspectives, Case-studies and Innovative Strategies. London: Routledge.

Schein, E. (1992) *Organizational Culture and Leadership*, 2nd edn. San Francisco, CA: Jossey-Bass.

Senge, P.M. (1990) *The Fifth Discipline: The Art and Practice of the Learning Organization*. New York: Doubleday.

Simpson, B. (1997) 'Representation and the Re-Presentation of Family: An Analysis of Divorce Narratives', in A. James, J. Hockey and A. Dawson (eds) *After Writing Culture: Epistemology and Praxis in Contemporary Anthropology*, pp. 51–70. London: Routledge.

Solomon, N. and McIntyre, J. (2000) 'Deschooling Vocational Knowledge: Work-based Learning and the Politics of Curriculum', in C. Symes and J. McIntyre (eds) *Working Knowledge: The New Vocationalism and Higher Education*. Buckingham: Open University Press.

Somers, M.R. and Gibson, G.D. (1994) 'Reclaiming the Epistomological "Other": Narrative and the Social Constitution of Identity', in C. Calhoun (ed.) *Social Theory and the Politics of Identity*, pp. 37–99. Oxford: Blackwell.

Tait, G. (2000) *Youth, Sex and Government*. New York: Peter Lang.

Tannen, D. (1990) *You Just Don't Understand: Women and Men in Conversation*. London: Random House.

Taylor, K., Marienau, C. and Fiddler, M. (eds) (2000) *Developing Adult Learners*. San Francisco, CA: Jossey-Bass.

Tennant, M. and Pogson, P. (1995) *Learning and Change in the Adult Years: A Developmental Perspective*. San Francisco, CA: Jossey-Bass.

Tisdell, E. (1998) 'Poststructualist Feminist Pedagogies: The Possibilities and Limitations of Feminist Emancipatory Adult Learning Theory and Practice, *Adult Education Quarterly*, 48(3): 139–56.

Treadgold, T. (2002) 'Love in a Hot Climate', *Business Review Weekly*, 17 January.

Trinca, H. (2001) 'The McKinsey Rapport', *Australian Financial Review*, 9 February.

Usher, R. and Edwards, R. (1994) *Postmodernism and Education: Different Voices Different Worlds*. London: Routledge.

Usher, R. and Edwards, R. (1995) 'Confessing all? A "postmodern" Guide to the Guidance and Counselling of Adult Learners', *Studies in the Education of Adults*, 27(1): 9–23.

Usher, R. and Solomon, N. (1999) 'Experiential Learning and the Shaping of Subjectivity in the Workplace', *Studies in the Education of Adults*, 31(2): 155–63.

Usher, R., Bryant, I. and Johnson, R. (1997) *Adult Education and the Postmodern Challenge*. London: Routledge.

Vattimo, G. (1988) *The End of Modernity: Nihilism and Hermeneutics in Post-modern Culture*, trans. J.R. Synder. Cambridge: Polity Press.

Voigt, K. (2002) 'Will Yoga Provide a Competitive Career Edge?', *Wall Street Journal Online*, www.careerjournalasia.com/myc/success/20020226-voigt.html, accessed 12 August 2002.

Wagner, P. (1994) *A Sociology of Modernity: Liberty and Discipline*. London: Routledge.

Waugh, P. (1992) *Practising Postmodernism/Reading Modernism*. London: Edward Arnold.

Weissner, C., Meyer, S. and Fuller, D. (eds) (2000) 'Challenges of Practice: Transformative Learning in Action', paper presented at the Third International Conference on Transformative Learning, Teachers College, Columbia University, 26–28 October.

Wexler, P. (1995) 'After Postmodernism: A New Age Social Theory in Education', in R. Smith and P. Wexler (eds) *After Postmodernism: Education, Politics and Identity*, pp. 56–80. London: Falmer Press.

Williams, C. (1993) 'The Politics of Nurturant Teaching', *Studies in Continuing Education*, 15(1): 50–62.

Willmott, H. (1993) 'Strength is Ignorance; Slavery is Freedom: Managing Culture in Modern Organizations', *Journal of Management Studies*, 30(4): 515–52.

Wonacott, M.E. (2001) 'Career Portfolios', *Practice Application Brief No 13*. Columbus, OH: ERIC Clearinghouse on Adult, Career, and Vocational Education, Center on Education and Training for Employment, The Ohio State University.

Woodward, K. (1997) 'Concepts of Identity and Difference', in K. Woodward (ed.) *Identity and Difference*, pp. 7–62. London: Sage.

Wruck, K.H. and Eastley, M.F. (1998) *Landmark Education Corporation: Selling a Paradigm Shift*. Boston, MA: Harvard Business School.

Yates, L. (1992) 'Post-modernism, Feminism and Cultural Politics, Or, If Master Narratives Have Been Discredited, What Does Giroux Think He is Doing?' (review essay), *Discourse*, 10(1): 124–33.

Yates, L. (1993) 'Feminism and Education: Writing in the 90s', in L. Yates (ed.) *Feminism and Education* (Melbourne Studies in Education), pp. 1–9. Bundoora: La Trobe University Press.

Yates, L. (1998) 'Constructing and Deconstructing "Girls" as a Category of Concern', in A. MacKinnon, I. Elgqvist-Saltzman and A. Prentice (eds), *Education into the 21st Century: Dangerous Terrain for Women?* London: Falmer Press.

Yates, L. (1999) 'Feminism's Fandango with the State Revisited', *Women's Studies International Forum*, 22(5): 555–62.

Yates, L. (2001) 'Subjectivity, Social Change and the Reform Problematic, *International Journal of Inclusive Education*, 5(2): 209–23.

Yates, L. and McLeod, J. (2000) 'Social Justice and the Middle', *Australian Education Researcher*, 27(3): 59–78.

Index